I MUST GO:

AN EPIC JOURNEY OF KNOWING GOD AND FINDING PURPOSE

D1521367

I MUST GO

An epic journey of knowing God and finding purpose

Jon Haley ⟨⟩ Michael Haley

CONTENTS

FOREWORD

Nearly ten years ago, I was flying over the mountains of Colorado, headed to preach at our student ministry's annual summer camp. I was looking forward to the week and had all my sermons ready to go, when the Spirit of God began to prompt my heart to reconsider what I had in mind to preach. This made me a bit nervous because camp was starting that evening and I typically work and preach best when I'm well prepared.

As we started our descent to land, I began to pray trying to discern whether it was God speaking to me or what I had for dinner the night before! I remember praying, "God, if this is from you, please give me the exact messages you want me to preach." I didn't want to blow it.

Growing up in church, I remember how important summer camps were. For me, they were "mountain-top experiences" in my walk with the Lord. I can look back on my life and see how God used summer camps void of distractions, and an intentional focus on his Word and worship to shape me spiritually. I wanted the students from our church to have the same type of experience.

Looking out the window of the plane praying, I sensed the still, small voice of God speaking to my heart. "Show them all I did on mountains in the Bible." And it hit me. I had never heard a sermon on it. I had never even read a book about it.

God was revealing to me in the moment he did some of his most amazing miracles and gave some of his most profound teachings on mountains. As I searched the scripture, I began to write down all these "mountain-top" moments in the Bible.

- Abraham showed he fully trusted God by marching his son, Isaac, up a mountain.
- God delivered the Ten Commandments to Moses from a mountain.
- Eljiah battled the false prophets of Baal on a mountain.
- Jesus taught his first sermon on the side of a mountain.
- He died on a mountain.
- He ascended from a mountain.
- He gave his Great Commission from a mountain.
- He will return to a mountain.

How had I missed this in all the years of studying the Bible? God has so much to teach us and we have so much to learn from the mountains of scripture.

This is why I am so grateful for Michael and Jon writing *I Must Go*. In this book, the Haley brothers take us on a journey of ascending various mountains in scripture revealing transformational truth for everyday valley living. I can't wait for you to allow them to be your guide as you make your way up some of these mountains.

You will be inspired.
You will be encouraged.
You will be challenged.

Remember one more thing as you begin this journey. Making the climb is not always easy, but it's *always* worth it. The view is incredible. You'll find this to be true, with every turn of a page.

Jarrett Stephens
Teaching pastor of Prestonwood Baptist Church
Author of *The Mountains Are Calling: Making the Climb for a Clearer View of God and Ourselves*

ACKNOWLEDGMENTS

Michael Haley

First and foremost, I want to thank God for providing me the opportunity to enjoy His creation each and every day. Hiking the JMT was truly an experience of a lifetime. I'm so thankful to God for giving me the mental, physical, and spiritual ability to conquer such a feat.

To my beautiful wife, Misti. Thank you for loving me so well. There is no one else I would rather have walking beside me on this trail we call "life." Your unconditional love and continued encouragement have molded me into the man I am. My prayer for our boys is they will find a treasure like the one God gave me. You have cheered me on from day one, and your cheers only seem to get louder as the years pass.

Mom and Dad, thank you for leading us so well. Your faithfulness to God has always been the same whether you were on the mountain or in the valley. You have left a legacy in your kids and grandkids which I pray will continue for many generations.

To my kids: Derek, Dustin, and Makena thank you for loving me despite my many failures as a dad. I pray you will spend your life doing everything you can to know God greater and fulfilling His purpose for your life. May you look at each new day as a faith adventure. My prayer for you is God would give you a double portion of the blessings and gifts He has graciously given your mom and me.

My sisters: Melissa Litke, and Amy Haley have always loved me and pushed me to be better. You both have experienced mountaintop moments as well as challenging valleys and have become stronger in your faith as a result. I'm thankful for you both and proud to call you my sisters.

Jon, our desire to compete with one another probably helped us get through the many tough days on the JMT. There is a bond between twins which cannot be understood by those who do not have a twin. I'm excited to continue to see how God uses you and your ministry. It has been fun working on this project together.

To the most amazing church, Cross Creek. Thank you for loving me and my family well. Thank you for the many who gave to the #FeedTheNeed cause. Your support in allowing me to get the needed supplies and to take three weeks off was amazing. You are a remarkable body of believers! May we continue to help people find and follow Jesus.

Thank you, Amy Howard, for proofreading, editing, and encouraging us through this process. Only a sovereign God could know and be able to orchestrate us three coming together 30 years later on this project. You are such an encourager.

Finally, I want to thank MANNA Worldwide for their God-sized vision. Thank you for allowing us to partner with you to help rescue kids around the globe from the grip of poverty. We not only get to feed empty stomachs, but we get to play a role in seeing helpless souls find healing.

Jon Haley

My first acknowledgment is to my Lord and Savior, Jesus Christ. God definitely gave me the strength in my legs and the air in my lungs for me to complete this epic journey through some of the most beautiful areas of God's creation.

To my training partner and beautiful wife, Joy. You are my rock and I am thankful for your support. You walked mile after mile with me as we trained in the summer heat of Texas. You endured countless conversations about food, calories, and blisters. Thank you for your constant love, support, and encouragement.

Mom and Dad, thank you for your constant prayers and encouragement. The example you have lived out in front of your kids and grandkids has left a legacy of faith that will outlive us all.

To my kids: Blake and Blaire. Thank you for your motivation. You both have motivated me to always be the best man of God I can. The hike was one of my greatest achievements but watching you both faithfully serve your church and your Lord is the highlight of my life.

My sisters, Melissa Litke and Amy Haley, I am thankful for your love and support. God has brought you both through many mountaintops and valleys. I am proud to be your brother.

Michael, we have pushed each other to be better our entire life. I am a better pastor, dad, husband, brother, and follower of Jesus because of you. Thank you for passionately following Jesus and leading your family.

To the greatest church, Hallmark Baptist. Thank you for your passion to lead people to find and follow Jesus locally and globally. Thank you for the many who gave to the #FeedTheNeed cause. Your prayers and financial support allowed me to make this once in a lifetime journey. I am humbled to serve you as your pastor.

To Amy Howard, the girl I mercilessly picked on in youth group thirty years ago. God has miraculously brought our lives back together to bring this project to completion. Thank you for correcting my many mistakes.

INTRODUCTION

It was a beautiful, warm, sunny day as we drove around the city of Havana, Cuba. We were visiting some local churches for possible ministry partnerships with MANNA WORLDWIDE. While sitting in the bus and talking shop with some other pastors and missionaries, I was asked a question. "You want to do something crazy and adventurous to raise money for children living in poverty?" Andrew Even (see pp. 203–207) had me at, "crazy and adventurous", so raising money for missions was the tipping point. Leaning across the aisle of the bus, I got the scoop on this amazing hike. I began to get a small glimpse of how remarkable of an opportunity this was going to be. While taking in the sounds and scenery of Cuba, he showed a picture listing statistics, which began to paint a picture of what this epic journey would hold. I had never heard of John Muir or the John Muir Trail, but that one conversation would lead me down a path to find out all I could about this unbelievable hike across the Sierra Nevada Mountain Range. The picture I was shown, which is still on my phone, had the number 47,000 at the top.

Under the number it says, "feet of total elevation gain." That is the equivalent of climbing Mt. Everest one and half times! I might not have known who John Muir was, but the adventurous part of me knew I was all in even with a limited amount of knowledge. Looking back, it might be beneficial I didn't really know what I was getting myself into. We all probably had that one friend as a kid who was always coming up with some kind of crazy scheme and part of you was hesitant, but the other part of you simply said, "I must go." You knew if you didn't go, you might miss out on an adventure of a lifetime. You would miss out on all the stories which would be told until you were at the phase of life where you met for coffee at McDonald's every morning to reminisce about the good old days. FOMO, Fear of Missing Out, is real and powerful, no matter your age. I'm reminded of a famous quote, which has often been falsely attributed to Mark Twain, *"Twenty years from now, you will be more disappointed by the things you didn't do than by the ones you did do. So, throw off the bowlines. Sail away from the safe harbor."*

John Muir was born on April 21, 1838 and his most famous quote is, *"The mountains are calling, and I must go."*[1] This quote was taken from a letter he wrote to his sister in 1873. I believe God created us with a sense of ad-

---

[1] John Muir to Sarah Muir Galloway, September 3, 1873, Yosemite Valley.

venture. We have this desire to explore, which stems from a desire to see all our Creator has created. It is a desire to know Him more and for Him to know us more. The inspiration for this book is from the 17 days my brother and I hiked with five other men, who became like brothers. We were able to raise over $100,000 to help rescue kids from the grip of poverty. We also gained an immense amount of inspiration and information from a book written by Jarrett Stephens called; *The Mountains are Calling*. We are going to look at nine different mountains in Scripture to see why God called these people to the mountain and what they learned when they answered God's call to make the climb.

Most Christians have a desire to see God and to experience what we have come to call, a mountaintop experience. Mountaintop experiences are not meant to be long term moments, although they can lead us toward a lifetime of movement and leave us with lasting memories. I've had the privilege of climbing 11 mountains that are over 14,000 feet. Ten of those are in my home state of Colorado. I conquered the 11th one while hiking the John Muir Trail. Mt. Whitney stands at 14,505 feet above sea level and is the highest point in the lower 48 states. People ask me all the time why I enjoy climbing mountains. Hiking or ascending a 14er is more of a love-hate relationship. Something in me has a hard time turning down an adventure and there is something magical about the views from high atop a mountain. When we think about God calling us to the mountain to experience Him in a new way, maybe we need to look at it in this light. God is inviting us on a faith adventure and the prize is we get to see Him. Some things in life will never get to be seen and understood unless you are willing to take that first step when God calls you to make a move. Mountaintop moments inspire us to know Him more, but the second part of that quest comes when we descend the mountain and share the information and inspiration with others. In this journey, we see the two main reasons God invites us to experience Him on the mountain. First, God desires to reveal Himself to us. Maybe we get a chance to experience a characteristic of God in a new way. Maybe it is an opportunity for us to be reminded of the identity of God. Maybe God just wants to show up and show off in your life. When God calls us to see Him, it is for our information. We see Him so we can learn more about who He is by understanding more about Him, we get to learn more about who we are. Secondly, I feel God calls us to the mountain so we can be inspired. When we get a proper perspective of God, it will allow us to also have a proper perspective of ourselves. Daniel Akin said, *"A true movement of God will cause the church to look up to heaven, catching a vision of his greatness; in to view our own desperate sinfulness apart from his grace, and out to the lostness of the nation's cut off from his goodness.*"[2] Mountaintop inspiration is two-fold. These moments inform us, but if that is all, we have missed half of the equation. The other half is we would come down from the mountain and share what we have learned so we can inspire others to make the climb. I believe part of the pull for me is also being able to experience and see things not everyone could see and experience. Large amounts of work and preparation goes into a mountaintop experience. Many people are simply not willing to make the sacrifices necessary to climb the mountain and see God in a new way.

Months and months of preparation led all 14 of us to the Cottonwood Lakes campsite where we would begin our journey. Nine of the 14 had planned and prepared to hike the whole trail, while five in our group were planning on hiking with us for five days. Our first night was filled with a lot of nervous excitement. Pastors, missionaries and business leaders; all of whom had little to no experience in a hike of this magnitude, would soon find out what they had gotten themselves into. Monday morning, August 20, 2019, I woke up filled with anticipation and excitement. Half a year of training, studying and preparing all led me to this point, and I could barely wait. I woke up, quickly packed up my gear, and headed to the trailhead. It was

[2] Daniel L. Akin, *10 Who Changed the World* (Nashville: B&H, 2012), 69.

around 6:30 a.m. when I got ready, but it wasn't until 8:00 a.m. before all 14 of us were assembled. The 17-day adventure began!

This first day was definitely a tough way to begin the journey. Most of our group was from what I call the" flat lands", which means there was no way for them to know how their bodies would respond to the elevation. We found ourselves hiking from around 9,500 feet that morning to over 12,500 as we went over New Army Pass. 16 miles on the first day was probably not the best plan, but it was one way to see who was and who was not prepared for this hike. Andrew and I took a side hike, while waiting on the rest of the group, and jumped into the freezing water of Soldier Lake. The top of Army Pass was covered in snow, which caused everyone to have to scramble in order to find the path to the top. The first two and a half days were, in retrospect, bonus miles. Due to the large group and the difficulty of getting permits for this hike, we had to hike an extra 22 miles just to start the official 222-mile hike. For months, we were all part of a Facebook group sharing thoughts on gear and training to inform and inspire one another. Guys were hiking mountains, walking bleachers, spending countless hours on stair climbers, watching YouTube videos of people who had hiked the trail, and many trips to the mega sports store REI. We had about five miles left on our first day, and several members of our team had lagged way behind. Many more were pleading with our fearless leader to set up camp and stop for the day. We had a rigorous 17-day schedule ahead of us, so to stop short on the first day would have been disastrous. A couple of us went ahead to try and find our campsite to hopefully message back to the guys, our first night of sleep was just a little further ahead. We learned on the first day, the last two to three miles of everyday were always going to be tough. We finally made it to Rock Creek Ranger station just before dark and quite a few people had already set up camp in the same spot. I stopped one guy and asked him where the best place for a group of 14 to set up camp would be, and he looked at me like I was crazy. He said, "There is not a spot here, but if you go another mile or two there is another campsite there." I knew I wasn't about to go another mile or two, and I definitely wasn't going to relay that information to the group behind me. We found a spot and set up camp. We arrived at the end of day one and it was already evident some were well prepared, and some were in serious trouble.

My identical twin brother, Jon, and I spent a lot of time together on the trail. Part of our time was spent discussing how we could share this adventure with others. Those talks led us to write this book together. As you read this book, our desire for you is to be willing to prepare yourself for God's call to climb the mountain. If you are not already prepared. We had no clue what this hike was going to hold for us, but we were willing to jump in and see. We pray as we both share our experiences; you will grow in your faith and your desire to ascend the mountains in your life. When God calls you on an epic journey of knowing and experiencing Him, with a prepared heart, mind, and soul; we believe you will be ready to answer by saying, *I MUST GO!*

Chapter 1—The Valley of Fear

Jon's Tale from the Trail

The cool, crisp air was seemingly blowing right through my recently purchased down-filled jacket. Being chilled to the bone was the least of my concerns, as I was preparing to go to bed. I set the alarm for 3:00 a.m., while next morning's challenge was consuming me with fear and anxiety. We were camping out for the third straight night at 10,000 feet of elevation. Sickness had overcome me most of the day. Anxiety about the possibility of failing to summit Mt. Whitney was palpable. The failure rate of those who attempt to climb Mt. Whitney is higher than the failure rate for summiting Mt. Everest. 70 percent of people fail who attempt to summit Mt. Whitney. Yes, you read that correctly. Mt. Whitney claims a 70 percent failure rate. The complete lack of preparation for the rigors and hazards of the climb, consistently remains the number one reason for failure to summit Mt. Whitney. Most people underestimate altitude effects and overestimate their level of conditioning. Some feel their resilient mental toughness combined with their heroic ignorance of any potential pitfalls, will win the day. Unfortunately, these dubious strategies put not only the strategists at risk, but also anyone obligated to rescue them. For example, a medevac with all the trimmings or fellow climbers already pushing themselves to their limits, would be required to risk their own lives to save an unprepared hiker.

Climbing into my borrowed mummy sleeping bag, led me to begin praying. Prayers for strength, endurance, and sleep; were at the top of my prayer list. I imagine you have experienced watching the hours slowly tick by, all while wanting to go to sleep. You lay there and think, if I fall asleep right now, I can get five hours of sleep. I laid in my tent, almost hyperventilating, while struggling to catch my breath. Was this a result of altitude? Anxiety? Or a combination of both? Most of my day on the trail was spent behind trees trying to vomit. Not being able to eat much because even the smell of food caused me to begin dry heaving, left me weak and worried. The cold walk to the exposed toilet, poached on a wooden platform with no walls and no roof, became way too familiar. I found myself sticking my finger down my throat multiple times, trying to relieve myself of whatever was making me feel so sick. Crying out to God all night, my prayers became more earnest as the hours slowly passed. Desperately wanting to crest Mt. Whitney, I begged God to allow sleep and healing. Several hours went by with no sleep. This felt like a spiritual battle, so I continued to plead with God to put Satan away from me and my thoughts. All night I wrestled with my pride and ego, because of my passionate desire to pinnacle the mountain. I wanted to complete this hike for hunger. The team had worked hard, prepared, prayed and raised a lot of money for the precious orphan kids who desperately needed a home.

The team leaving at 4:00 a.m. gathered outside my tent, so I asked them if we could pray. I confessed to them the spiritual battle I had been fighting all night and at times I didn't know if I was wrestling with Satan or God. Two of the other men told me they had a similar experience in their tent that night. We circled up and prayed for God to give us air in our lungs and strength in our legs. We began the journey with the resolve God had brought us here and He was not going to leave us here. The spiritual battle in the valley prepared me for the challenge of the mountain. I found myself making the journey up the mountain one step at a time, one breath at a time, while my friend Keith stayed one step behind me the whole way uphill. When I rested, he rested. When I took a drink of water, he took a drink of water. I would stop to catch my breath and apologize for taking another break. He had the same reply every time, *"It's ok Pastor, you got this."* Later, he told me he intentionally called me Pastor all day to let me know he looked up to me. He believed it would give me courage to keep going. The journey for me started at 4:00 a.m. and ended that night at 6:00 p.m. The 7.6-mile journey up the mountain took me eight long hours, while the 7.6-mile journey back down the mountain took me six hours. The God who reassured me in the valley, was the God who blessed me on the mountaintop. I will never forget the exhilaration of climbing to the top of the mountain or the exhaustion of wrestling God in the valley. Psalm 23:4 has never meant more to me than it did that sleepless night in the tent. Even though I walk through the valley of the shadow of death, I will fear no evil, for you are with me; your rod and your staff, they comfort me. Never forget God is with you. He is with you in the valley. Because of His perfect strength, you can endure the valley and enjoy the mountaintop.

Michael's Tale from the Trail

We had slept in a beautiful and amazing campsite at
the Crabtree Ranger Station. This would be the only time
on the hike we would keep our same campsite for two
nights in a row. Day two was a shorter day, so we could
rest a little in preparation for Mt. Whitney. As mentioned
before, this is the highest peak in the lower 48 states, standing at 14,505 feet. Some of our group woke up at 4:00 a.m.
to get a head start, while some left at 6:00 a.m. Then there
were a few in our group who chose to stay behind to rest.
Some were nursing some behemoth blisters, others were
ailing from horrible knee pain, and a couple were struggling with altitude sickness. I experienced my worst night
of sleep that night due to stomach issues, which woke me
up several times during the night, causing me to take the
long walk to the bathroom spot that my brother described
earlier. These walks would affectionately become known
as "The Walk of Shame." Our hike for the day would be
over 15 miles, while ascending over 4,200 feet in elevation. All the while, knowing we would be returning down
that same 4,200 feet to arrive back at our campsite for the
night. During the hike up Mt. Whitney, I was overcome
thinking how often in our lives we celebrate the God of
the mountains, but we fail to realize He is the same God
in the valley. Valleys by nature are low. Valleys are where

the fights happen. Valleys are where we let fear and doubt enter. No one looks forward to the valley. I believe if we change our perspective, we can celebrate who God is, while in the valley. Valleys are where giants are slain. Valleys are where we walk through the shadow of death, but without fear, because He is with us. Many times, it is in the valley when our faith is made real. It is in those low points of life, when we get to see and experience God in a whole new way. Maybe, we should look at valleys as the new mountaintop experience.

The Valley of Fear

Before we begin climbing mountains, I want us to take a walk through the valley. Whether you grew up with flannel graphs, sword drills, Vacation Bible School and Jr. church or not, you are probably familiar with the story of David and Goliath. I'm not one known to look for fights, but I'm also not known as one who would run from a fight. In the story of David, we see that the Philistines are on one mountain and on the other mountain the Israelites are trembling in fear. In between these two mountains, we see the Valley of Elah, where the showdown between a shepherd boy and a champion warrior would take place. First Samuel 17:3–4 says,

> And the Philistines stood on the mountain on the one side, and Israel stood on the mountain on the other side, with a valley between them. ⁴ And there came out from the camp of the Philistines a champion named Goliath of Gath, whose height was six cubits and a span (1 Samuel 17:3–4).

While reading through this story for probably the 100th time, something stuck out to me like never before. David wasn't looking for a fight. He was curious as to who this pagan Philistine was who would defy the living God, but David was simply bringing supplies to his three oldest brothers. David inquired about what would be done for the man who defeated Goliath. His oldest brother, like most older brothers, preceded to put him in his place. He not only allows everyone within earshot, to know David was just a shepherd, but he was the shepherd over just a few sheep. David was simply asking a question, but his brother's fear and shame caused him to lash out at him. I don't think David was looking for a fight that day, but when he noticed no one else would stand up to fight this pagan, this fight became his fight. While reading this story, we see word gets back to King Saul, so Saul sends for David. I love the confidence David has as he enters the presence of the King. "And David said to Saul, 'Let no man's heart fail because of him. Your servant will go and fight with this Philistine'" (1 Samuel 17:32).

Sometimes the call to enter the presence of God is a call to come off the comfort of the mountain and to walk down into the valley where the giants reside. David knew he wasn't a giant warrior. David knew how Goliath towered over everyone. David knew what his brothers thought. David knew the odds were stacked against him. David knew what awaited him in the valley. David knew that the King had zero confidence in him. David also knew the Lord who delivered him from the paw of the lion and the bear, would deliver him from the mighty mitts of this nine-foot giant. David thought he was simply delivering a care package, but God was about to use him to deliver a nation. What paralyzed the army of Israel? What kept them on the safety of the mountain and out of the danger of the valley? It is easy for us to minimize their faith while maximizing their fear, but how many times in our own lives do we get stuck in mediocrity? How many times in our own lives do we choose to stay comfortable? How many times in our own lives do we focus on the size of the giant? It is so easy to stare at the giants in our lives and lose sight of how big our God is. Do you remember singing the children's song, "Our God is so big, so strong and so mighty, there's nothing our God cannot do"?

In the face of defeat, we really get to experience the thrill of victory. For 40 days, the nation stood in fear because of what awaited them in the valley. Often when we are faced with a spiritual battle, the battle is won and lost in our minds. As David did, we must remind ourselves in seasons of doubt, of the past faithfulness of God. We must remind ourselves God is the same in the valley as He is on the mountain. When we can remember this, we are able to say or even sing this song by Hillsong UNITED with conviction.

> So I will praise You on the mountain,
> And I will praise You when the mountains in my way.
> You're the summit where my feet are,
> So I will praise You in the valleys all the same.

O how high would I climb mountains,
If the mountains were where You hide.
O how far I'd scale the valleys
If You graced the other side.[1]

Let's finish the story as we look back to the valley.
First Samuel 17:45–47 says,

> Then David said to the Philistine, "You come to
> me with a sword and with a spear and with a jav-
> elin, but I come to you in the name of the LORD
> of hosts, the God of the armies of Israel, whom
> you have defied. This day the LORD will deliver
> you into my hand, and I will strike you down and
> cut off your head. And I will give the dead bod-
> ies of the host of the Philistines this day to the
> birds of the air and to the wild beasts of the earth,
> that all the earth may know that there is a God in
> Israel, and that all this assembly may know that
> the LORD saves not with sword and spear. For the
> battle is the LORD's, and he will give you into our
> hand."

David wasn't blind or ignorant to the battle in front of
him. He was very aware of the size of the giant. He was
very mindful of the sword the giant yielded. He saw with

[1] Joel Houston & Benjamin Hastings, "Highlands (Song of Ascent),"
Hillsong Music Publishing, 2018.

his own eyes the size and the magnitude of the weapons and the warrior in front of him. David found victory that day because he was also very aware of the God who would fight with him. "We must learn to get our eyes off the 'giant' in our life and onto the God over our life, like David did."[2] When we know God is calling us out of our comfort zone and into the battle, we can be confident He will fight with us and for us. It is with this kind of conviction we can show up to a sword fight with a slingshot. It is with this kind of confidence, we can come down from the mountain and head to the valley with the courage to simply say, *I MUST GO!*

---

[2] David Jeremiah, *Overcomer: 8 Ways to Live a Life of Unstoppable Strength, Unmovable Faith, and Unbelievable Power* (Nashville: Thomas Nelson, 2019), 18.

CHAPTER 2—PROVISION FOLLOWS OBEDIENCE

Jon's Tale from the Trail

The Bible is very clear on obedience leading to God's provision. However, obedience requires surrender and surrender requires humility. This creates a problem for me. Humility does not come natural for most of us. Clearly, the Bible calls us to live a life of humility. Humility is a must if we are going to live in obedience.

> **Philippians 2:3–5,** Do nothing from selfish ambition or conceit, but in humility count others more significant than yourselves. Let each of you look not only to his own interests, but also to the interests of others. Have this mind among yourselves, which is yours in Christ Jesus.

Jesus humbled himself and became obedient to the point of death.

> **Philippians 2:8–9**, And being found in human form, he humbled himself by becoming obedient to the point of death, even death on a cross.

Therefore God has highly exalted him and
bestowed on him the name that is above every
name.

Hiking 17 days, 244 miles, and over 47,000 feet; of
elevation gain will humble you. I was humbled many times
and in many ways. A few weeks before the hike began, I
was at the gym working out and trying to get in the best
shape possible. It was a normal Saturday and the leg workout had been average intensity, at best. I was in the middle
of a set of step-ups, when an intense stabbing pain entered
my right knee. The pain immediately caused me to quit
the workout and retreat to my house. Thankfully, I was not
scheduled to preach the following day because walking up
the stairs of the stage was almost impossible. A member
of my church, an athletic trainer, was examining me for
the second time on the conference table located in my office on a different Sunday after I had finished preaching.
I saw the look on his face. I could see his disappointment
and the angst. The news he was about to tell me was not
good. Fearful, I asked, "What is it?" He said, "I am confident you have a torn meniscus." The moment he said it, I
was devastated. I assumed this meant I could not make the
hike. Long story short, I went to two different doctors and
the second one gave me a cortisone shot. She told me this
will either work or it won't. Thanks!

The above story was all background to let you know about the moment on the hike, when I felt the most humbled. The day had been one of the longest days of the trip. We had planned to hike two passes in one day. The people who heard about our attempt to hike these two passes were mostly surprised, with a hint of, "WOW! You guys are stupid." Day seven proved to be a very tough day. The total miles in front of us after an early wakeup time, was 14.5 miles. Day seven would consist of a total ascent of 2,725 feet with a total descent of 3,638 feet. We climbed Pinchot Pass early in the morning, which tops out at 12,107 feet. Getting to the top was one thing, but then had to go down. This was a long five-mile 2,000-foot descent. In chapter five, my brother will inform you of the news we received at the bottom of the valley, while eating lunch and filtering water by the stream. The tragedy was trickling down the mountain to all the hikers. The task was now to climb from 10,153 feet of elevation to 12,094 feet to the top of Mather Pass, with heavy hearts and heavy packs. Palisade Lake is where we were headed. It seemed as if we would never make it. We were all using the Gut Hook app to track how far we had gone and how far it was to our destination for the day. The lake never seemed to get any closer. As we approached the lake, we received a text message through our Garmin inReach communicator. The message simply said, "We are all the way on the other side of the lake." Generally, this wouldn't have been a big deal, but this was not a normal lake. This was not a leisurely walk around a beautiful lake. This was a hike around, over, and through granite boulders which towered over the lake. (Google Palisade Lake JMT images.) I was so eager to be done climbing. I was beyond ready to finish the day and get into my tent. This extra walk around the lake added another two miles to an already long day. Michael and I tried to hurry, but I was extremely fatigued. I had not been able to eat an adequate lunch that day and was completely exhausted. The sun was setting, and we were desperately wanting to be at camp before darkness fell. The last mile was proving to be very difficult when suddenly, we saw a familiar face heading toward us. Lonnie (see pp. 126), a fellow hiker, was coming back to check on us. Lonnie let us know we only had a mile left until we reached camp. He offered to carry my backpack, as he could see I was struggling to make it. Pride swelled up in me and the answer was, "No, thank you." Shortly after I pridefully said "No", things changed. One simple step like the previous 20,000 steps that day, yet this one felt as if someone had shoved a knife into my left knee. Stumbling and almost hitting the ground, Lonnie knew something was wrong. I assured him I was fine. God reminded me humility is necessary and required. He had provided someone to help me and my pride kept me from accepting the provision God gave me. Humbling one's self is never easy, but it is always necessary. Lonnie took my pack and carried it the last mile of that long strenuous day and we made it before dark. As we look at Abraham and Mt. Moriah, remember obedience leads to provision. Surrender leads to obedience, and humility is required to surrender.

Michael's Tale from the Trail

We began day five with our packs a little lighter since this day would be our first resupply. Resupplies are a bittersweet necessity. While it is necessary to get more food, this also means your pack was going to get heavier. We made the climb to Kearsarge Junction, where we met up with the mule train carrying our food for the next seven to eight days. The heavy pack coupled with the afternoon sun, made Glen Pass a very intense climb. Once we completed the ascent, we came to our beautiful campsite. Rae Lakes campsite was an amazing peninsula, surrounded by a glass-like turquoise lake with a granite mountain backdrop. Several of us got in the freezing water to rinse off and to give our muscles some much needed cold-water therapy. While hiking day after day, I was constantly reminded that climbing a mountain came with a bill. Many people miss out on mountaintop experiences simply because they are not willing to pay the ransom necessary to get to the top. When we planned for the hike, we all assumed we could conquer each day by itself. We were concerned about the cumulative toll on our bodies. The only way to simulate this kind of extreme activity is to actually do it. Repeatedly, I heard people talk about how eventually you would get your trail legs, and I honestly found this to be true. The first five or six days, we would all wrestle with experiencing leg cramps in the middle of the night. Eventually, I no longer worried about whether my hamstring would knot up while I was unpacking my gear in my tent, leaving me to scramble and straighten out my leg as soon as possible. Muscle memory is an incredible thing. Our muscles eventually adjusted to what we asked of them each day. Think of your faith as a muscle. When you exercise your faith, it will eventually become stronger. Walking by faith and in obedience to God, we get to see firsthand, the faithfulness of God. Taking those steps of faith is frightening, but it becomes easier the more you do it. Faith memory is a real thing. The best predictor of God's future faithfulness is his past faithfulness. Maybe your faith is weak simply because you haven't exercised it an awhile.

Mount Moriah

When God called Abraham to the mountain, he called him to do the unthinkable. The call to climb Mt. Moriah was preceded by years of God proving Himself faithful to Abraham, but this was a seemingly impossible task. Let's look at the beginning of the story to see how Abraham ended up on top of a mountain, with a knife raised high above his head as he prepared to sacrifice his only son Isaac. His call from God came at an age when most people are dreaming of slowing down and enjoying retirement, while making frequent visits to spoil their grandkids. Abraham and Sarah had no children, although like most women, Sarah had dreamed for years of having children of her own. God invited them on a journey no one could or would have predicted. This adventure would begin with a huge step of faith requiring them to leave everything and everyone behind to follow a God they barely knew. What would they learn that would lead Abraham to be willing to make such a sacrifice?

Genesis 12:1–3 says,

Now the Lord said to Abram, "Go from your country and your kindred and your father's house to the land that I will show you. And I will make of you a great nation, and I will bless you and

make your name great, so that you will be a blessing. I will bless those who bless you, and him
who dishonors you I will curse, and in you all the
families of the earth shall be blessed."

Many of the promises of God are conditional, which means
we have a responsibility to uphold. We do our part, then
God will do His part. I believe all His promises are "Yes"
and "Amen", but many of those are predicated on our
"Yes" and "Amen." God promised to make a great nation
from Abraham and Sarah, if they were willing to leave the
known behind and follow God into the unknown. We will
see repeatedly in the life of Abraham and all throughout
Scripture, God's provisions follow our obedience. God returned to Abraham in chapter 13 and in chapter 15, to reas-
sure Him of the promise He had made to him in chapter 12.
The original promise from God came when Abraham was
75. 25 long, drawn-out years passed before God's promise
was fulfilled. God has blessed me and my wife Misti, with
three wonderful children. He gave me a child in my 20's,
30's and then in my 40's. I can't begin to imagine having
one when I was 100! Abraham trusted God, but his faith
was not perfect. Several times in his life he got ahead of
God, but ultimately, his faith made him righteous. His 25-
year journey with God eventually led him to the ultimate
test. Let's look at the first two verses in Genesis 22:

After these things God tested Abraham and said to him, "Abraham!" And he said, "Here I am." He said, "Take your son, your only son Isaac, whom you love, and go to the land of Moriah, and offer him there as a burnt offering on one of the mountains of which I shall tell you" (Genesis 22:1–2).

When God calls you to the mountain, a cost will always be required. It might be easy for us to read this and not really think about it, because you probably know the end of the story. Take a moment and really imagine the price or sacrifice God is asking Abraham to make. My wife and I had prayed for years for our second child and the answer we got was either "No" or "Not yet." One day we found out my wife was pregnant. We were beyond ecstatic, but a week later we received the tragic news the baby had died. When the doctor told us the news, he also told us the date our baby's heart stopped beating. We realized just a day after we found out she was pregnant; the baby was gone. Why in the world would God do this or allow this to happen? Sometimes God summons us to the mountain with an invitation into intimacy with Him. Knowing God intimately requires us to lay everything else on the altar of sacrifice. What is it in your life that would be the hardest thing for you to lay on the altar? What is it in your life that is off limits to God? What is it in your life that you really don't trust giving to God? If you are not willing to lay your stumbling block on the altar, that person or thing is keeping you from knowing God in a greater way. This is the area in your life where you really don't trust God. How Abraham responded in verse three after what God asked of him, will always amaze me and encourage me to live with greater faith.

> So, Abraham rose early in the morning, saddled his donkey, and took two of his young men with him, and his son Isaac. And he cut the wood for the burnt offering and arose and went to the place of which God had told him (Genesis 22:3).

I assume Abraham didn't sleep well that night, but when the sun arose, he got up and began the impossible climb to the top of Mt. Moriah.

Walking with God, like Abraham, is a daily decision to walk in obedience. When we choose to walk in obedience, we see walking by faith is not always easy, but always worth it. Walking in obedience allows us to see the amazing provisions of God. Abraham's long journey led him to the foot of Mt. Moriah. This long, hard journey began with one step of faith. Isaac and Abraham would begin the climb together. While Isaac had no clue what lay ahead, Abraham had faith they would come down from the mountain together. Let's continue to read in chapter twenty-two.

> When they came to the place of which God had told him, Abraham built the altar there and laid the wood in order and bound Isaac his son and laid him on the altar, on top of the wood. Then Abraham reached out his hand and took the knife to slaughter his son (Genesis 22:9–10).

Abraham had seen the provision of God over and over in his life, which allowed him to do the unthinkable. With arm raised high and heart sunk low, he was willing to sacrifice his only son in order to continue his life of faith and obedience.

> But the angel of the LORD called to him from heaven and said, "Abraham, Abraham!" And he said, "Here I am." He said, Do not lay your hand on the boy or do anything to him, for now I know that you fear God, seeing you have not withheld your son, your only son, from me (Genesis 22:11–12).

Abraham was willing to give it all to God. What Abraham learned, and what we see through this story, is God's provisions follow our obedience. When God makes a promise, we can trust He will always prove himself faithful to fulfill His word. I love how once God tells him to stop, immediately Abraham saw the ram caught in the thicket. When we walk in obedience to God, God's heart is moved, which opens our eyes to the provisions of God. Abraham understood God was a God of provision in his head, but it was on the mountain he understood God's provision with his heart. When you follow God to the mountain, you will find He is your perfect provision. When you follow God to the mountain, you will understand the heart of God more intimately. It is one thing to know the promises of God, but when we walk in obedience, we get to experience the provisions alongside the promises. Ultimately, there is one question we need to wrestle with if we are going to climb the mountain of sacrifice. Is a life of surrender to Him worth it? Abraham climbed the mountain and named the place, "The Lord Will Provide." Abraham would say, YES, it is worth it. *I MUST GO!*

Chapter 3—Preparation Precedes Presence

Jon's Tale from the Trail

I am not a planner or a detail-oriented person by nature, which proved to make the preparation for this hike a little overwhelming at times. I often worked out twice a day, attempting to get into the best shape of my life. I walked with a full 35 lb. pack many days to work and backpack in the 100-degree heat of Texas. I lost 35lbs (my pack weight) in preparation for this amazing challenge on which we were about to embark.

An unforgettable scene unfolded on day five. Hiker buffet was in full effect. Food was being traded, bartered, and scavenged. Hikers we didn't know, joined the fray and were grateful for the bounty of food being freely bestowed upon them. The setting was chaotic, exciting, and a little crazy. Let me see if I can shed some light on the scene.

The bear canisters we carried our food in, hold a max of seven days of food. The hike was 17 days. I am guessing you can figure out the math doesn't add up in this equation. You cannot simply drive up to the trail and drop food off to someone. Only a few places on the trail exist, in which you come across any civilization. The two-day walk-in trail we had, created extra planning. The first place we could have mailed food ahead was MTR (Muir Trail Ranch), which we would not reach until day ten. You will read more about MTR at the end of this chapter from my brother. Ten days was way too long, so this caused a dilemma in trying to plan on how to get food. Keith, the friend who helped keep me motivated while we hiked Mt. Whitney, found a place with a mule train. A cowboy would ride out to us with our food packed on the backs of the mules. The cost for a group to pay for mules proved to be cheaper than mailing it to MTR or Reds Meadow. Keith volunteered to drive all our food from Texas to California. He dropped the food off the day before we started the hike, left the van in that location, and took a shuttle to meet us. I wish I could explain to you the amount of planning and preparation it took to get food for seven guys into six five-gallon buckets. Each hiker had to carefully plan out what they would eat and how they would get it to fit in the five-gallon bucket, then mail it to Texas in time for us to load them in a van to be driven to California. If that sounded confusing, "GOOD!" I want you to get a glimpse of how much coordination and organization it took to make this hike happen.

We were excited on day five to take a short five-mile downhill hike to meet the mules at Kearsarge Junction. We were anxious to see our TEXAS-FLAGGED five-gallon buckets with our resupply. Craig (see pp. 187–191) had been suffering from altitude sickness since New-Army Pass on day one. Craig exited the trail earlier that morning to meet Keith at Onion Valley where the van had been parked. Because we had a hiker leave, we had an extra supply of food. A feeding frenzy was created, which we affectionately called our hiker buffet. Every hiker was already sick of their own food, so this produced an exciting few minutes of food swap. One of our fellow hikers, Joey Candillo, (see pp. 192–195) came into the hike following the KETO eating plan. He intended on continuing to stay on the low-carb diet the entire hike. However, I gave him one of my homemade granola bars on day four, which I could no longer stomach. The sugar rush he experienced ended that plan quickly. Our hiker buffet would not have taken place without a great deal of preparation and planning. The parallels of our hike and our spiritual lives are unbelievable. Preparation for a thru-hike is vital and so is preparation in our spiritual journey. A "thru-hike" is to hike an established end-to-end hiking trail or long-distance trail with continuous footsteps in one direction. The point is preparation precedes presence.

Michael's Tale from the Trail

Day ten would be another long day on the trail, which was our earliest day to hit the route. With headlamps on, we were all eager to start the morning. We were excited because we were headed to Muir Trail Ranch, known to hikers as MTR. We started from Evolution Lake, headed down to McClure Meadow, and then walked along Evolution Creek. This was going to be a 16-mile day, with most of it being downhill. Downhill hiking is bittersweet on the JMT, because you knew this meant an inevitable big climb was coming. Morale was high that morning but was fading quickly. Worried about the health of my brother and the morale of the group, I spent a good portion of the day texting back and forth with my wife. MTR was a place where you could pick up extra supplies and ravage the hiker boxes for surplus food. It is amazing how almost every snack I packed became repulsive to me after about four days, so the hiker boxes were something I anticipated. My wife was able to call the ranch and find out they had just enough cabins for our group to be able to sleep in a bed for the night. After ten nights of sleeping in a tent on an air mattress, which sounded like someone was wrinkling up a bag of chips every time you rolled over, a bed sounded incredible. In addition, we had a place to wash our clothes, even if it was only a bucket with some soap, and a chance to take a warm shower. We also found out paying for a cabin came with a hot dinner, hot breakfast and a sack lunch for the tough 3,000-foot ascent up Seldon Pass ahead of us on day 11. Finally arriving at MTR, we couldn't get to our rooms soon enough. Once my clothes were washed and hung up to dry, I headed to the Hot Springs pool, where I experienced a glimpse of the glory of God. I wish my words were eloquent enough to describe the setting for this experience. I say experience, because that is what this moment was. Not having showered or really washed for ten days was a new encounter for me. With my feet swollen, blistered and caked in dirt; I spent a lot of time scrubbing them with soap in the wonderful 106-degree spring water. As I stood inside this rock wall with the beauty of the mountains as a backdrop, I poured bucket after bucket of hot water over me. Once I got the first five layers of dirt off my body, I slowly climbed into the huge hot springs pool. The only reason I got out of the pool was because I was hungry and a hot, homemade, fresh dinner awaited me. MTR by far, was my favorite place on this hike. The lasagna we had that night can only be described as heavenly. Nine straight nights of dehydrated food will cause you to appreciate a good meal like never before.

Mount Sinai

Red River, New Mexico, is one of my Mom and Dad's favorite places to visit. I remember taking vacations there as a child, and my parents still love to visit this wonderful little resort town nestled in the Sangre de Cristo Mountain Range. In June of 2019, our whole family planned a vacation there for my parents 50th wedding anniversary. My brother and I thought while we were there, it would be advantageous to take a practice hike. We would be heading for the Sierra's in just two short months, so a hike with a fully loaded pack in the elevation of New Mexico sounded like a smart idea. I'm not sure about the name of the trail, but it was longer and tougher than either one of us were mentally prepared for that day. It was a beautiful morning and the hike was going according to plan, as we enjoyed the crisp mountain air. We were about five miles into the hike when things began to get a little sketchy. Looking back, we should have turned around at this point and considered it a good practice run. We crossed over this small bridge and the trail went cold. There was so much snow, the trail was no longer visible. For some reason, New Mexico doesn't seem to believe in putting signs up in the middle of the trail to help with directions. Call it stubbornness or perseverance, which neither one of us has a shortage of, so we kept going. This character trait would prove handy for

Jon while we were on the JMT. My brother's phone had the trail map on it, but his battery was running low. He kept putting it in airplane mode to try and conserve power. We would turn on the GPS and look for the red dot indicating whether we were headed in the right direction. Time after time, we would head in the course we thought was correct, only to turn the phone back on and recognize we were way off course. Countless times we both fell in waist deep snow. This was the first time I had used my trekking poles, which proved to be valuable in assisting me in my quest to get up out of the deep snow. After several hours of treading through waist deep snow, we made it to the top of the trail. The map showed the trail basically made a loop, so we searched and searched for the trail, which was nowhere to be found. We climbed up to the top of a rock wall and realized there was nothing but a sheer cliff on the other side. We had a decision to make. Do we head back the way we came, or go in the direction that the map showed the trail went? We knew what it meant to return the way we had come. Deep snow, wading through ankle deep freezing water running under a blanket of snow, and a hidden trail awaited us. After praying and some moments of anxiety, we decided the known was better than the unknown. Tired and deflated, we made the long trek back down the trail. At least for the trip down we could retrace our footprints left in the snow. Once we finished the long trek down, we took a closer look at the map, which was located at the trailhead. This map had the trail scratched out, confirming what we had come to understand at the top of the climb. The trail no longer made a loop. Thankfully, we made it back just in time for our parents 50th wedding anniversary dinner, and a search party was unnecessary. That hike was beneficial in preparing us mentally and physically for the trek of a lifetime. It confirmed the physical training we had been doing was working, but there was still more preparation to be done. Hiking across 12 mountain peaks over 17 days is not something you should enter without adequate training.

Moses was saved providentially by the hand of the man's daughter, who was trying to kill him, along with every other Hebrew boy. For the first 40 years of his life, Moses learned what it meant to live as a somebody. He lived with privilege in the palace. The next forty years, Moses lived as a fugitive and it was there, he learned to live as a nobody. After an encounter with God at the burning bush, Moses would spend the next 40 years learning what God could do with anybody willing to believe God could use a nobody. Moses' first encounter with God took place on a mountain. Later, God invited Moses back up this mountain to reveal the Ten Commandments to him and establish a covenant with the nation, known as the children of Israel. As you read through the Old Testament, you realize entering the presence of God was not something you did half-heartedly or on a whim. Many days on our JMT journey, I was overcome with emotions just soaking in the presence of God while enjoying His creation. Knowing you are seeing and experiencing something most people can only dream about, is eye-opening and inspirational. We all desire mountaintop moments with God, but we cannot manufacture these moments. You cannot manipulate the presence of God into your life. We can do things to prepare ourselves to experience His presence, but many times we fail to truly make the effort to prepare our hearts for the presence of a Holy God.

God reveals Himself to Moses in Exodus chapter three. Moses was simply going about his day when God showed up. Exodus 3:1 says,

> Now Moses was keeping the flock of his father-in-law, Jethro, the priest of Midian, and he led his flock to the west side of the wilderness and came to Horeb, the mountain of God.

Mt. Horeb is more commonly known today as Mt. Sinai. Many mountaintop moments come from the mundane moments in our lives. The mundane can become a mountaintop when God is involved. Let's look at this call a little closer.

And the angel of the Lord appeared to him in a flame of fire out of the midst of a bush. He looked, and behold, the bush was burning, yet it was not consumed. And Moses said, "I will turn aside to see this great sight, why the bush is not burned." When the Lord saw that he turned aside to see, God called to him out of the bush, "Moses, Moses!" And he said, "Here I am." Then he said, "Do not come near; take your sandals off your feet, for the place on which you are standing is holy ground" (Exodus 2:3–5).

Moses responded to God's invitation the same way Abraham did. Isn't this the response we all pray we have when God shows up in the mundane moments of our life? "Here I am", or "I must go" is our desire, but is it always our reply?

My biggest fear for the hike became a reality on a training hike just a few weeks before the big journey began. Joey, (aka KETO) and I decided to go on a shakedown hike in Rocky Mountain National Park. We were going to camp out two nights to test our gear and our conditioning. Being from Missouri, Joey was excited to get some elevation training in, since it is not something you can simulate in Missouri. We had just begun our five-mile hike which would eventually lead us to our campsite for the night, when half a mile in, I was suddenly on the ground. Having horribly weak ankles, my biggest fear was rolling my ankle on the hike and having to somehow limp off the mountain unable to complete the JMT. This training hike had brought all those fears to the forefront of my mind. The ankle ended up being uninjured. When I fell, I realized I had never fallen with trekking poles before, so I wasn't quite sure how to catch myself. My right elbow took the brunt of the fall and I was bleeding profusely. My ten-year-old son Dustin was terribly concerned after seeing his dad take a nasty spill. I later found out Joey doesn't do well with blood and he was struggling to keep himself from fainting. We got the elbow patched up a little and made it to our campsite for the night. This was a great reminder a basic first aid kit was a necessity and worth the extra ounces of weight. The scar on my right elbow is a reminder to me preparation is necessary, but sometimes painful.

Let's fast forward to Exodus 19, where we see God is ready to introduce himself to the wandering, whiny nation. The children of Israel had heard all about the God of Abraham, Isaac and Jacob. They had heard the stories of this God who had made a covenant with Abraham. The plagues were a powerful visual of the commanding God who had rescued them from slavery. Seeing the Egyptian army drowned in the Red Sea, was evidence of

His prevailing power. Up to this point, they understood the power of God, but now were being invited into the presence of God. This was more than being guided by a pillar of fire or a pillar of cloud. This was an invitation to come into His presence personally.

> **Exodus 19:9–12**, And the LORD said to Moses, "Behold, I am coming to you in a thick cloud, that the people may hear when I speak with you and may also believe you forever." When Moses told the words of the people to the LORD, the LORD said to Moses, "Go to the people and consecrate them today and tomorrow and let them wash their garments [11] and be ready for the third day. For on the third day the LORD will come down on Mount Sinai in the sight of all the people. And you shall set limits for the people all around, saying, 'Take care not to go up into the mountain or touch the edge of it. Whoever touches the mountain shall be put to death.

We learn here the nation had to prepare themselves before they could enter the presence of God. It is a privilege to come before the God of the universe. What was God teaching them there at the foot of Mt. Sinai? What can we learn about God here at the base of the mountain? We learn two

important truths about the character of God from this encounter with God. First, God is Holy. God is not like you.
God is not like me. God is completely different and whol-
ly separate from His creation. *"We know nothing like the
divine holiness. It stands apart, unique, unapproachable,
incomprehensible and unattainable. The natural man is
blind to it. He may fear God's power and admire His wisdom, but His holiness he cannot even imagine."*[1] Let's look
at the definition of the word Holy. "The root word means
to divide, to mark off, to set apart from all else; it's the
opposite of profane. To be holy is to be different, distinct,
or unique from the common or ordinary."[2] The best way I
can describe the holiness of God is by thinking back to my
childhood growing up in Tornado Alley. Tornadoes will
leave you in awe, all while having a good measure of fear.
The power of a tornado is amazing to see, but at the same
time, it is healthy to fear. Second, we learn God is glorious. *"God is so glorious that even the mountains quaked
and shook in His presence"*[3] Isaiah 6:3 tells us the whole
earth is full of His glory. Have you ever caught a glimpse
of the glory of God? Living in Colorado Springs, I get a

[1] A.W. Tozer, *The Knowledge of the Holy: The Attributes of God*
(New York: HarperOne, 1992), 103.
[2] Chip Ingram *The Real God: How He Longs for You to See Him*
(Grand Rapids: Baker, 2016), 121.
[3] Jarrett Stephens, *The Mountains are Calling: Making the Climb
for a Clearer View of God and Ourselves* (Colorado Springs: Multnomah,
2018), 63.

preview of His glory every morning when I look out my kitchen window and see Pikes Peak. Sunsets and sunrises are another peek at His glory revealed here on earth. While working on this chapter earlier tonight, my six-year-old daughter climbed into my lap for some cuddle time. It was then, I shut the computer and we went upstairs to lay down on the couch and snuggle under a blanket while watching the rest of *The Emperor's New Groove*. What a foretaste of this glory we can experience every day, if we are paying attention.

Why do we avoid the presence of God? If we look at the first five verses of Isaiah chapter six, I think we can see what keeps us from taking the time to prepare so we can enjoy His presence. Isaiah 6:1–5 says,

> In the year that King Uzziah died I saw the Lord sitting upon a throne, high and lifted up; and the train of his robe filled the temple. Above him stood the seraphim. Each had six wings: with two he covered his face, and with two he covered his feet, and with two he flew. And one called to another and said: "Holy, holy, holy is the LORD of hosts; the whole earth is full of his glory!" And the foundations of the thresholds shook at the voice of him who called, and the house was filled with smoke. And I said: "Woe is me! For I am

lost; for I am a man of unclean lips, and I dwell in the midst of a people of unclean lips; for my eyes have seen the King, the LORD of hosts!

A proper view of God will always give us a proper view of ourselves. His glory revealed has a way of unveiling our lack of glory. His holiness exposed has a way of revealing our unholiness. Isaiah saw the glory of God and his only natural response was the realization he was unclean. When we come close to God, we will be aware of our sinfulness, which is a good thing. The recognition of His holiness needs to fuel us to run to the mountain, rather than from the mountain. Just like the nation of Israel, we must prepare ourselves to come to God. How do we prepare or consecrate ourselves? If you have never put your faith in Christ, you need to receive the truth; Jesus is the only way. Salvation is not about a religion to follow, but a relationship to receive. God knew you and I could never measure up to His holiness, so He sent his Son Jesus to redeem us. Just like he set the nation of Israel free from slavery, He has made a way for you to be set free from your sin. I would assume most of the people reading this book would call themselves Christians, so the encouragement for you is to prepare your heart before you enter into the presence of God. We know as children of God we can come boldly to the throne, but that is only because of the completed work of Jesus. As I mentioned earlier, my greatest fear or concern on the hike was stepping on the side of a rock and spraining an ankle. Many days when I was coming down from the mountain, I was reminded of how we should enter the presence of God. While scurrying over boulders and racing down rocky trails, I repeated a phrase in my head over and over. The mantra I proclaimed was, "Step with confidence, but don't get cocky." This statement, for me, sums up how we should come boldly to the throne. Coming into the presence of God with a flippant attitude is not something God takes lightly. Think about Uzzah, who reached out his hand to balance the Ark of the Covenant. Uzzah was struck down immediately. Do you remember the married couple who schemed together to lie to God about the offering they were giving? The men had just returned from taking out Ananias' body when they heard the thump of Sapphira hitting the ground.

What made the night at MTR so glorious and highly memorable, is what I had experienced leading up to this day. When we enter the presence of God with a hungry and desperate soul, there is nothing more glorious or fulfilling than sitting at the feet of Jesus. Can you see the spiritual parallel? Isn't that what an encounter with the Holy and glorious God does? He takes us in our sin and filth and washes us white as snow. Paul tells us in Romans it was while we were still sinners, or still in our sin, Christ died for us. We don't clean ourselves up in order to come to Him. We come to Him and He makes us new. We come to Him and He exchanges our filth for His righteousness. We come to Him and he exchanges our heart of stone for a heart of flesh. We come to Him and He exchanges our death for His life.

Ascending the mountain of God is a privilege, but we must be sure we don't approach this mountain without preparation. May we strive to be prepared every day to meet God on the mountain when He calls us. When He calls, may we run to him with confidence and not from Him in contrition. May our hearts be prepared and ready so that when he calls, our answer is, *I MUST GO!*

Chapter 4—Monotony in the Valley

Michael's Tale from the Trail

While taking a 17-day hike across the mountains, one of the things quickly learned is you settle into a monotonous routine. I found it took me about an hour and a half each morning to do everything I needed to do to be ready to take off with the group at the designated time. The first thing I did every morning was the same thing I normally do every morning when I wake up. Being in the mountains just made this chore a little more difficult than usual.

Morning Monotony:

1. Bathroom.
2. Get Dressed.
3. Let the air out of my air mattress, role it up and put it away.
4. Get my snacks and lunch packed and put in my backpack.
5. Put medicine on my feet and re-bandage all the blisters.

6. Reluctantly get out of my sleeping bag and put it away.
7. Scoot to the edge of the tent and force myself to put on my shoes and socks. By day 7 my feet were enjoying some enormous blisters, so putting the shoes back on was the last thing I wanted to do.
8. Filter a couple bottles of water for breakfast and for the start of that day's journey.
9. Cook my oatmeal and sit on the very uncomfortable bear canister while enjoying my hot breakfast.
10. Pack up my tent.
11. Make sure everything was situated in my backpack and then it was time to hit the trail.

One of the many running jokes and songs we sang on the trail was Sonny and Cher's song, *I Got You Babe*. In the movie, *Groundhog Day*, the character played by Bill Murray is woken up day after day after day at 6:00 a.m., with the same song playing on his alarm clock. I'm guessing as you read these lyrics you will have to fight the temptation to not sing them.

> Then put your little hand in mine
> There ain't no hill or mountain we can't climb
> Babe, I got you babe
> I got you babe.[1]

[1] Written by Sonny Bono, Performed by Sonny & Cher. July 4, 1965.

There were not too many mornings you wouldn't hear someone, normally me, singing this song from the warmth and comfort of their tent, while trying to convince themselves they could get up and do it all over again.

Jon's Tale from the Trail

The valley represents suffering, trials, testing, persecution, and pain. God tested Elijah in the valley so he could be trusted on the mountain. The thrill on the mountaintop is more palatable after the monotony in the valley. Hiking the JMT was not a life-long goal for me. Researching the JMT, led me to understand many people do have this hike and this experience as a life-long pursuit. Day after day, we had the same conversations with hikers from all over the world. They were shocked to learn all of us were rookies with very little experience. Many of them had worked their entire life for this moment. Feeding kids all over the world was the driving force of our team. Conquering poverty was our motivation to conquer these mountains.

The hike brought on challenges for me I didn't anticipate or expect. The pace we set was fairly optimistic, even for avid hikers. Andrew and I spent hours at a local burrito restaurant in our hometown, mapping out the best possible route that would allow us to finish in 17 days. However, the days proved to be longer and more difficult than we realized. I am not sure what I was dealing with, but I was sick for at least ten of the 17 days. I struggled many days to find the energy to get up the mountain and simply finish the day. To say the routine became monotonous, would be an understatement. Each day, I would wake up at 4:30

a.m. to get everything packed up and begin hiking by 6:00 a.m. Hike up a mountain and then hike back down. Arrive at camp at around 5:00 p.m. and set up the tent. Filter water so I could cook a meal. Strive for an hour to eat half a bag of ramen noodles without throwing up. Filter more water to drink in the night and to be prepared for breakfast. Climb into my bed exhausted, tired and desperate to feel better the next day.

I was tired and weak due to my lack of nutrition. My plan was to eat around 5,500 calories a day, but I had only been averaging around 2,000 calories a day, if I was lucky. I couldn't really eat much food, because I couldn't keep it down. The moment I put food into my mouth or smelled the food, my body would reject it. God allowed me to eat breakfast most days and one morning, I ate ramen noodles and mashed potatoes to ingest as many calories as possible. I would eat a bite and then dry heave. Eat another bite and then dry heave. This process lasted about ten days. Trust me when I say the routine became wearisome.

God taught me a lot in the valley on this hike. God taught me to trust Him completely. God showed me He is always with me, no matter the situation. The level of desperation I felt inside my tent some nights is hard to convey. I vividly remember on day eight sitting in my tent at 5:00 in the afternoon as it hailed. I had tried to eat, but once again it was a futile effort. I have a video on my phone of me in the tent talking about throwing up as the hail peppered my tent. It was at that moment, I realized that my tent had a hole in it. Thank God I had taped duct tape to my trekking poles for just such an occasion. God brought me through the valley so my faith in Him and His ever-present grace would become more real in my life. Peter said it this way.

> **1 Peter 1:6–7,** In this you rejoice, though now for a little while, if necessary, you have been grieved by various trials, so that the tested genuineness of your faith—more precious than gold that perishes though it is tested by fire—may be found to result in praise and glory and honor at the revelation of Jesus Christ.

Mount Carmel

Routine is closely related to monotony. The same ole', same ole', day after day, doing the same thing. Elijah is most known for his battle on top of Mt. Carmel. I was blessed in December of 2019 to stand on top of the same mountain where Elijah stood. I could see for miles and miles in all directions and the view was absolutely breathtaking. I was humbled by the reality I was standing at the same place where Elijah called down fire from Heaven. Ironically, one of the funniest things I saw on our tour through Israel was a sign posted on a fence on top of Mt. Carmel. The sign was a "no campfire" sign. Sorry, but I thought that was hysterical. It was funny enough to take a picture of and post all over social media. However, before Elijah would call fire down on the mountain, he would go through the fire in the valley.

We are not privy to much information regarding Elijah. The Bible does not go to great lengths to give us his family history or a detailed resume of his past experiences. James briefly mentions him in the New Testament and states he was a man just like us. He was an ordinary man who God used in an extraordinary way. However, God took time in the valley to prepare him for the mountain.

Elijah's name was not without significance. During the period of the Old Testament, the prophet's names most

often had symbolic meanings. Elijah was born into a time
in which Israel was not known for worshiping the God
of Abraham, Isaac, and Jacob. In fact, they were known
for worshiping many false gods. However, Elijah was
born for such a time as this. Elijah means, "My God is
the Lord" or "Jehovah is the Lord!" Like many other Old
Testament figures, his name declared the purpose of his
life. Remember though, before he could call the fire down
on the mountain, he would have to walk through the fire
in the valley.

> **1 Kings 17:1–7**, Elijah the Tishbite, of Tishbe in
> Gilead, said to Ahab, "As the Lord, the God of
> Israel, lives, before whom I stand, there shall be
> neither dew nor rain these years, except by my
> word." And the word of the Lord came to him:
> "Depart from here and turn eastward and hide
> yourself by the brook Cherith, which is east of
> the Jordan. You shall drink from the brook, and I
> have commanded the ravens to feed you there."
> So he went and did according to the word of the
> Lord. He went and lived by the brook Cherith
> that is east of the Jordan. And the ravens brought
> him bread and meat in the morning, and bread
> and meat in the evening, and he drank from the
> brook. And after a while the brook dried up,

because there was no rain in the land.

Did you catch what the Lord said? He told Elijah to go down to a brook called Cherith. Hold that thought. Back up a minute. Read verse one again. "Elijah the Tishbite, of Tishbe said to Ahab". God sent a nobody to tell the King it was not going to rain until Elijah said it would.

Ahab was King of the Northern Kingdom. King Solomon was the last king to lead the United Kingdom of Israel. After King Solomon died, Israel entered a prolonged civil war which divided the nation into two kingdoms. The Northern Kingdom was known as Israel and the Southern Kingdom was known as Judah. Judah, the Southern Kingdom, would have 20 different kings reign over them, and less than half of the kings were known as followers of God. The Northern Kingdom did not have one single leader who followed Jehovah God.

King Ahab had permitted his wife Jezebel to bring the worship of Baal into Israel (16:31–33) and she was determined to wipe out the worship of Jehovah (18:4). Baal was the Phoenician fertility god who sent rain and bountiful crops, and the rites connected with his worship were unspeakably immoral. Like Solomon who catered to the idolatrous practices of his heathen wives (11:1–8), Ahab yielded to Jezebel's desires and even built her a private temple where she could worship Baal (16:32–33). Her plan was to exterminate the worshipers of Jehovah and have all the people of Israel serving Baal.[2]

You can get a glimpse of the battle starting to brew. Elijah, whose name means, "The Lord is Jehovah", finds himself telling the King Jehovah is going to judge the nation and specifically his reign over the nation. Jezebel was determined to rid the nation of this same Jehovah. The stage was being set for the battle on Mt. Carmel.

> God wonderfully suits men to the work he designs them for. The times were fit for an Elijah; an Elijah was fit for them. The Spirit of the Lord knows how to fit men for the occasions. Elijah let Ahab know that God was displeased with the idolaters, and would chastise them by the want of rain, which it was not in the power of the gods they served to bestow.[3]

Let's get back to the brook where we left Elijah. God told Elijah to go to the brook called Cherith. The word

[2] Warren W. Wiersbe, *Be Responsible: Being Good Stewards of God's Gifts* (Colorado Springs: Cook, 2002), 127.
[3] Matthew Henry, *Matthew Henry Concise Bible Commentary* (Peabody, MA: Hendrickson).

Cherith in the Hebrew language means "to cut off or to cut down."

> The imagery is that of a tree being chopped down at its base, and this is what God was doing with Elijah during his time at Cherith. God wanted to eliminate Elijah's pride and self-reliance. Like cutting down a tall tree, God humbled Elijah's that he could then use him in a mighty and powerful way.[4]

God sent him through the valley of preparation before he could scale the mountain of celebration. During this time of preparation, Elijah would learn to trust God. He would rely on the most disgusting bird; a raven, to bring him food. Every day he would wait morning and night for the ravens to bring him his daily bread. I can't imagine the monotony of waiting each day for the birds to show up with the rations. The routine my brother talked about earlier in this chapter became tedious. Luckily, it was only 17 days and we had people who were there experiencing it with us. I was shocked at how many people hike the JMT by themselves. I am not sure I could have handled the re-petitiveness by myself. We don't know exactly how long Elijah was at Cherith. All we are told; is he was there until

[4] Jarrett Stephens, *The Mountains are Calling: Making the Climb for a Clearer View of God and Ourselves* (Colorado Springs: Multnomah, 2018), 17.

the brook dried. God then commanded him to pack up and head down the trail.

> **1 Kings 17:8–12**, Then the word of the Lord came to him, "Arise, go to Zarephath, which belongs to Sidon, and dwell there. Behold, I have commanded a widow there to feed you." So he arose and went to Zarephath. And when he came to the gate of the city, behold, a widow was there gathering sticks. And he called to her and said, "Bring me a little water in a vessel, that I may drink." And as she was going to bring it, he called to her and said, "Bring me a morsel of bread in your hand." And she said, "As the Lord your God lives, I have nothing baked, only a handful of flour in a jar and a little oil in a jug. And now I am gathering a couple of sticks that I may go in and prepare it for myself and my son, that we may eat it and die."

"Another place with a name of significance, Zarephath comes from a word that means 'to melt or to smelt.' Elijah went from being cut down to being melted."[5] Elijah went from depending on the ravens to bring him food, to depending on a poor widow and her son with a food supply as dry as the brook he just left behind. Many times, we are

[5] Stephens, *The Mountains are Calling*, 17.

not invited to the mountain because we fail to trust Him during the monotony in the valley. Day after day, Elijah was reminded of the fact God was all He had. In the end, he realized God was all he needed. We all want to experience the mountaintop, but we must be willing to stay faithful and resilient while we are stuck in the valley. It's now time for Elijah to put into practice on the mountain what he learned in the valley—GOD IS TRUSTWORTHY.

> **1 Kings 18:20–21,** So Ahab sent to all the people of Israel and gathered the prophets together at Mount Carmel. And Elijah came near to all the people and said, "How long will you go limping between two different opinions? If the Lord is God, follow him; but if Baal, then follow him." And the people did not answer him a word.

Elijah drew the line in the sand and asked them a question. "How long will you go limping between two different opinions?"

Are you going to follow Baal or God? The next line in verse 20 is alarming. "And the people did not answer him a word." It is startling how loud silence can be. Their silence was deafening while simultaneously speaking volumes. King Ahab was leading them away from God and Elijah was calling them to a point of decision. He is calling them to stop wavering between Jehovah God and the Baal. He was pushing them to make a commitment. They were silent! Elijah switches his focus from the wavering nation to the false prophets. The prophet looks to them and explains the challenge. Let's look at the challenge.

> **I Kings 18:23–24,** Let two bulls be given to us and let them choose one bull for themselves and cut it in pieces and lay it on the wood but put no fire to it. And I will prepare the other bull and lay it on the wood and put no fire to it. And you call upon the name of your god, and I will call upon the name of the Lord, and the God who answers by fire, he is God." And all the people answered, "It is well spoken."

The prophets of Baal went from morning to evening, crying out to their false gods to burn the sacrifice, but nothing happened. Elijah began to make fun of them and continued to incite them. Finally, Elijah has had enough, and he speaks.

> **1 Kings 18:30–39,** Then Elijah said to all the people, "Come near to me." And all the people came near to him. And he repaired the altar of the Lord that had been thrown down. Elijah took twelve stones, according to the number of the

tribes of the sons of Jacob, to whom the word of the Lord came, saying, "Israel shall be your name," and with the stones he built an altar in the name of the Lord. And he made a trench about the altar, as great as would contain two seals of seed. And he put the wood in order and cut the bull in pieces and laid it on the wood. And he said, "Fill four jars with water and pour it on the burnt offering and on the wood." And he said, "Do it a second time." And they did it a second time. And he said, "Do it a third time." And they did it a third time. And the water ran around the altar and filled the trench also with water. And at the time of the offering of the oblation, Elijah the prophet came near and said, "O Lord, God of Abraham, Isaac, and Israel, let it be known this day that you are God in Israel, and that I am your servant, and that I have done all these things at your word. Answer me, O Lord, answer me, that this people may know that you, O Lord, are God, and that you have turned their hearts back." Then the fire of the Lord fell and consumed the burnt offering and the wood and the stones and the dust, and licked up the water that was in the trench. And when all the people saw it, they fell on their faces and said, "The Lord, he is God; the Lord, he is

God." And Elijah said to them, "Seize the prophets of Baal; let not one of them escape." And they
seized them. And Elijah brought them down to
the brook Kishon and slaughtered them there.

"Elijah went through his refining in Cherith and Zarephath. God knows the trials and tough times have a way
of purifying our faith and solidifying our trust in Him.
This is why he led Elijah through the pain and suffering
and why we go through pain and suffering today."[6] We
must realize a faith which has not been tested, is a faith
which cannot be trusted.

Elijah came out of the valley understanding God was
trustworthy. I exited Yosemite Valley accomplishing an
unbelievable 244-mile journey with a greater understanding of the trustworthiness of God. When God calls me
through the next valley, because of what I learned in this
one, my answer will be, *I MUST GO!*

[6] Stephens, *The Mountains are Calling*, 63.

CHAPTER 5–
INTIMACY REQUIRES INTENTIONALITY

Jon's Tale from the Trail

I spent hours and hours watching YouTube videos about thru-hiking. I was one of the least experienced hikers in the group and I wanted to be prepared. While I watched various experts in the field of hiking, I learned quite a bit. Successful hiking requires intentional planning. Details are essential and attention to every detail is imperative. You would be shocked how many hours you can watch on how to prepare your food. You would be disgusted by the videos I watched regarding blisters and foot care. However, they did prove to be a big help. Let me share with you one crucial element of the hike: FOOD!

Hikers are not allowed to hike the JMT without a "bear canister". A bear canister is a bear-proof plastic container, all your food and scented toiletries must go into at night. The purpose is to keep the bears out of your tent at night while you are trying to sleep. The bear canister has a limited amount of space in which to pack all your food.

Hours and hours of packing, weighing, and recalculating were required to understand how to make your food fit. The bear canister can hold up to seven days of food at a time, if you pack efficiently. The goal was to get seven days of food, with an average of 5,500 calories per day, in this plastic container. You wanted to get as much food in the can as possible, all while weighing as little as possible. My goal was for the canister not to weigh more than 14 pounds. Planning, preparing, and detailing each meal and every snack to reach the lowest weight and highest calorie count, was mind-numbing. My wife, Joy, was tired of hearing about how one brand of granola had a higher calorie count per ounce than another one. I even found a recipe online on how to make a high-calorie granola bar. I made at least three different batches to test the recipe. I was shocked at how good they tasted and how high they were in calories. Each bar weighed about four ounces and contained over 700 calories. Intentional planning is vital to a successful thru-hike. Similarly, intentionality is required if we are going to experience intimacy with the Lord.

Michael's Tale from the Trail

We got up a little earlier on day seven, because we had two passes, we were planning to conquer. Pinchot and Mather Pass stood in our way before we could finish the 14.5-mile trek to Palisade Lakes. Today would bring a little more clarity to exactly what we got ourselves into by signing up for this hike. This would be one of the longest days on the hike for me. My brother was still struggling with sickness and it became evident early on, this was going to be a tough day. It was about 1:00p.m., so I stopped at a beautiful water crossing and ate my lunch. I tried to choke down my peanut butter and jelly-filled tortilla, but my stomach just wasn't having it. Once Jon caught up, he stopped to eat, and we heard the tragic news. A man who was going over the same pass we were about to go over, had fallen and died earlier that morning. Falling with a 40-pound backpack can turn a simple fall into a tragedy. We would later learn, some of the guys in our group were there when the helicopter first landed to investigate the incident. While standing on the side of the mountain face, my brother and I stopped and spent some time in prayer for whomever had fallen and their family. In that moment of prayer, we were both reminded of the sacrifices our own families made for us to be on this journey. Every guy in our group wrestled with whether this hike was worth it, considering death was a possible reality on this mountain. We knew the hike was going to take us out of our comfort zone, but the certainty of the dangers present, became glaringly evident. The reality being, no way off the trail existed, was cemented in our minds as we listened to the helicopter circle above our heads. I remember the fear coming over me as I crossed the snow-packed area which had caused the accident just hours before. Normally this small stretch of snow would have not concerned me. Therein, lies the danger of becoming comfortable. Too many Christians have settled into a comfortable Christian life and when we really examine Scripture, those two don't coexist. When we get too comfortable in our walk with Christ, it can cause us to lose focus and intimacy in two ways. First, we lose sight of the dangers of sin which can easily cause us to slip and lose our footing. Second, we can get so comfortable we no longer really need Christ. If we are not stretching our faith by taking steps in our walk that do scare us a little, then we really aren't walking by faith.

Mount Desolate

The details matter in our lives. They matter in our physical lives as we take care of the temple God has given us. They matter in the lives of our kids. They matter in our spiritual lives. Intimacy with God doesn't just happen. Intimacy with anyone doesn't just materialize. Intimacy only comes with intentionality. We must be intentional in our walk with Christ if we are going to grow in our sanctification. Many examples can be found in the New Testament of Jesus getting away from the crowds to spend time with His Father. Here are a few verses which speak to this truth.

> **Mark 1:35**, And rising very early in the morning, while it was still dark, he departed and went out to a desolate place, and there he prayed.
>
> **Mark 14:23**, And after he had dismissed the crowds, he went up to the mountain by himself to pray. When evening came, he was alone.
>
> **Luke 5:15–16**, But now even more the report about him went abroad, and great crowds gathered to hear him and to be healed of their infirmities. But he would withdraw to desolate places and pray.

Luke 6:12, In these days he went out to the mountain to pray, and all night he continued in prayer to God.

We see Jesus got away to the mountain and to desolate places to pray, reflect, and renew His mind. "Jesus prayed before choosing his disciples. He prayed on a mountain before Peter's great confession of faith and before He walked on water. He went up to a mountain to pray with His inner circle of disciples before He was transfigured before them. "He went to a 'certain place,' to a mountain and his disciples saw Him, followed Him, and asked Him to reach them to pray."[1] Jesus routinely withdrew himself from the crowds to pray. Think about that. If Jesus needed this time alone with the Father, how much more do we need it? One of the many traps Christians can easily fall into is having a knowledge of God, but lacking intimacy with Him. A head knowledge of God, without a heart knowledge, will leave you dry and empty. We need to build routines in our lives so we can be intentional with our intimacy. David says in Psalm 34:8, "Oh, taste and see that the Lord is good! Blessed is the man who takes refuge in him!" How often do we really take time with God to taste and see that He is good? The idea of this verse is we would try Him

---

[1] Jarrett Stephens, *The Mountains are Calling: Making the Climb for a Clearer View of God and Ourselves* (Colorado Springs: Multnomah, 2018), 72.

and experience Him. When you really try God or experience God, you will see He is good. I am going to be honest with you. I struggle big time with this! I struggle with intimacy with God. When I think of how David said he thirsted after God like a deer thirsts for water or how Paul wrote he wanted to know Jesus and the power of his resurrection, I find my desire for Him lacking. We all desire the mountaintop experience, but those moments only come when we take the time to truly know God. In his book, *The Mountains Are Calling*, Jarrett Stephens shares three enemies of intimacy. Most of us would claim we want to know God intimately, but we have allowed these enemies to creep in and keep us from really knowing Him. These enemies of intimacy can be found in all our relationships. If you are missing intimacy with your spouse, kids or any of your relationships, there is a great chance at least one of these enemies has got their foot in the door.

1. Busyness

Have you ever noticed how guilty we can feel when we think others might have the opinion, we are not busy enough? You know when you get a phone call and you are half asleep and the person on the other end of the call says, "Oh, did I wake you?" Immediately you change your voice, sit up, clear your throat and say, "Oh no I'm awake." We have somehow equated busyness with effectiveness, but that isn't always the case. If we are not careful, we can let our calendars dictate our Christlikeness. After reading Jarrett Stephens book, I was challenged to come up with a set of core values that I can use as a filter. Filters are meant to filter out things deemed either harmful or unnecessary. Filters on the John Muir Trail are your lifeline. My core values are things I want people to say about me when I have left this temporary tent behind. I want to attempt to filter my life through these three things:

1. Followed Christ
2. Family was led and loved
3. Finished Strong

In my own strength I cannot and will not live out these values but can when I lean into Christ and am intentional with intimacy. I believe His Spirit will empower me to live these. Don't allow the enemy of busyness to keep you from knowing God.

2. Complacency

Merriam Webster's Definition of complacency is, "marked by self-satisfaction especially when accompanied by unawareness of actual dangers or deficiencies."[2] How often does this define our walk with Christ? You will naturally drift away from God rather than towards God.

[2] "Complacency." Merriam-Webster.com. Merriam Webster, 2011.

Therefore, intimacy must be intentional. Ask yourself a few questions to see if you have started drifting down the mountain and away from Him, rather than striving to climb the mountain to know Him.

Complacency Test:

Is my worship authentic? If you find yourself only being able to worship God when your favorite song comes on the radio or is played on Sunday morning, there is a good chance you have just fallen in love with the worship of worship. Authentic worship is a lifestyle we live, and not just a song we sing.

Is my service enthusiastic? We are never more like Jesus than when we serve. Serving others is an outflow of intimacy with God.

Is my prayer life vibrant? The disciples asked Jesus to teach them to pray and I believe the reason for that was they saw how He prayed. Prayer is powerful, and they saw the power it gave Jesus. Oswald Chambers said, *"Prayer does not fit us for the greater work; prayer is the greater work."*[3]

Is my faith being stretched? We know without faith it is impossible to please God, so we must constantly be moving forward. We cannot allow ourselves to become comfortable. When was the last time you shared your faith

---

[3] Oswald Chambers, *My Utmost for His Highest* (1935).

with someone? When was the last time you took a step of faith?

3. Comfort

Climbing a mountain is not easy. Many times, we fail to climb the mountain simply because we are comfortable where we are in life. When we become comfortable, it can cause us to become unwilling to pay the price to know God in a more intimate way. Salvation is free for us, but it came at a high price for Jesus. While salvation is free, sanctification is a call to take up your cross daily to follow Him.

A call to intimacy is a call to get out of your comfort zone and climb the mountain to really taste and know God is good. Are you willing to eliminate busyness, guard yourself from complacency and pay the price to keep from getting too comfortable to enjoy intimacy with the Savior? When God calls you to leave your comfort zone, my prayer is your desire to experience God in a new way will lead you to say, *I MUST GO!*

CHAPTER 6—PRAYER PRODUCES POWER

Michael's Tale from the Trail

One of the toughest things for me while on the hike, was being away from my family for three weeks. With two days spent getting there, and an additional two days traveling home, we were apart for 21 days. We all had plenty of pictures of our families to look at while we were on the trail, but as you know, a picture just isn't the same. There is a certain phase in your kids' life where being the tickle monster is your number one job as a dad. My youngest is in this phase right now. She will run by me and scream, "The tickle monster can't catch me." Most of the time we end up in the kitchen on opposite sides of the island, playing a game of cat and mouse. Eventually, the monster prevails, and she is on the ground or the couch laughing uncontrollably. I tend to grow my beard out, but it doesn't normally stay long before I shave it. There is a short window of time during the beard-growing phase which is optimal for tickling the neck of your kids. All three of my kids have had different names for this segment of beard growth. My oldest, for some reason called it "Musketeering." Don't ask me where he got that from, because I don't have any clue. Ten years later we tried to use the same name for our second child, but he ended up turning it into "Mouseketeering." Imagine a five to six-year-old boy saying, "Dad, don't musketeer or mouseketeer me". Fast forward another five years and my daughter has come up with her own word, which is a little closer to being more descriptive of what it might feel like. She will say, "Dad, I don't want your splinters." Being the tickle monster is one of the best roles you can have as a dad. When we think about prayer and the opportunity, we must come to our Heavenly Father. I wonder how differently we might approach prayer if we pictured Him as a loving daddy.

Prayer on the hike was something we spent a lot of time doing and enjoying. Several times my brother and I would spend some time just talking to our Creator out loud together, while walking the trail and taking in His beautiful creation. Each time, we were overcome with emotion. The whole group spent time each morning in prayer before hitting the path. Many prayers were offered up for those who were struggling with sickness. One of my prayers was for God to keep my blisters from getting infected. Infected blisters were the last thing I wanted to take me off the course, but it became a concern for me. We spent time praying for kids living in third world countries, who are desperately in need of clean water. We had a visual reminder of their need every time we sat down to filter our water. The filters we used are the same type of filters many of us have carried door to door in villages in Honduras and Guatemala. MANNA has provided us the opportunity to give these filters to families who are in desperate need of clean water.

Day 12 was one of our longer days, which I know we have said often. Many times, we thought we were set up to have an easy day, but we quickly learned they were all going to be hard. On this particular day, we had a big descent. We also added a few miles from our original itinerary so we could shorten the distance for day 13. Day 13 was going to take us into Reds Meadow, where we would pick up our last re-supply and enjoy a tasty cheeseburger. Going downhill on the trail became much more painful than climbing for me. It was on this day; my right leg was ready to give up. The muscle right above my kneecap, which I'm assuming is part of the thigh muscle, was nearing its end. Every step down was met with excruciating pain. My trekking poles were used to try and help keep as much weight off this leg as possible. Going down boulders, I would have to stop and use my left leg to jump down and then catch myself with the same leg. Those last two miles felt like they would never end. Most of the last five days of our hike were spent coming down the mountain. Thankfully, someone had an Icy Hot patch, so putting one of these on became part of my morning ritual. My prayers on the last two miles of every hike became more intense with every painful step.

One of the beautiful things about God is we can come to Him in prayer with anything at any time. His love for you is greater than the love of any father for his children. You may have had an amazing father, you may have had a missing father, or you may have had an abusive father. No matter what the image of your earthly father is, you can be assured that our Heavenly Father is perfect and His love for you is based on who He is and not on what you've done. I love my kids, but I am far from being a perfect dad. Sometimes, my kids come to me and are met with someone who is too busy staring at his phone to listen to them. Sometimes my kids come to me and are met with anger or selfishness. Other times, my kids come to me and are met with an inability on my part to meet the need they have. You will never come to God and be met with anything other than a God who hears, cares and is fully capable. The power in prayer is not to move the heart of God, but to be moved to the heart of God.

Jon's Tale from the Trail

I am not sure I could pinpoint which day caused me the most fear while on this adventure. I don't typically live with a spirit of fear, but this journey brought new and unfamiliar fear into my soul. The inability to communicate with my family was a source of frustration, as well. The solar panel phone charger which dangled from the back of my pack did not work as well as advertised. Keeping our phones and the Garmin inReach satellite communication device was of utmost importance. However, both were dying, and it was filling me with anxiety. I experienced a two-day period where the struggle of hiking was so strong, the ability to charge these devices became secondary. Climbing into my tent exhausted, hungry, cold, and fearful was a real occurrence many nights. Truthfully, communicating with my wife came with mixed emotions and with unintended consequences. The few times I did text her seemed to make me more homesick and less confident. Two different nights, around day five and six, I yelled out of my tent to my brother and asked him to have his wife text my wife. I wanted her to know my phone was almost dead, and to tell her I was safe. I desperately wanted to have a conversation with her, but I chose not to. Thinking through the psychology of that decision is, as they say, above my paygrade. However, spiritually speaking, it makes me do a little soul searching. Do I respond to God the same way? Is it possible, the times I need him the most, are the times I feel the most isolated and fearful? Does Satan put doubts in my mind which cause me to not communicate with God, when it is the very thing most needed?

I recorded a video of myself on day 13 and was able to upload it that day as we entered Reds Meadow. The video was scary. The church back home was praying for all of us and they knew I had been sick. The video they saw was confirmation I was not doing well. I looked terrible and the video only made my wife and everyone in my church worry more. We stayed in a condo that night, which was fantastic. I ate several pieces of pizza and they tasted divine. I finally got to see my wife's face via FaceTime. The thought of getting off the trail was still very real. As I laid on the floor that night, I prayed for God to allow me to get a good night's rest to feel confident that finishing the trail was the right choice. I had cold sweats all night, so sleep evaded me. The next morning brought more doubt, fear, and uncertainty. God used Facebook to change my mind. There were about 50 people from my church family who commented, letting me know they were praying for me. The power of prayer was evident. Their prayers for their pastor motivated me. Day 14 of the John Muir Trail gave me a new perspective. God was working through the prayers of those who loved me. Prayer is a conversation based on a relationship. Their prayer was based on their relationship with their friend and with their Lord. The moment I read all their comments, I knew I could and would finish this hike. James tells us the prayer of a righteous person is powerful, and that verse came alive for me in a new, profound way.

Mount Eremos

I have been asked multiple times if I would ever hike the JMT again. The first month after I got back from the hike, my answer was an emphatic "NO!" I almost died out there. I noticed after about four to six weeks my resounding "no" began to soften. Two months removed from the hike and my answer was, "I might think about it." As I type this, six months have passed since the trek which could have taken my life. I now wonder, dream, and contemplate: if I had the time, money, and cause, would I do it again? A few months after finishing the hike someone asked me the familiar question, "Would you do it again?" I tried explaining to them, it seems the farther I get away from it, the more likely it seems I would do it again. He referred me to a book entitled, *The Power of Moments* by Chip and Dan Heath. Let me share an excerpt from their book.

Consider an experiment in which participants were asked to undergo three painful trials. In the first, they submerged their hands for 60 seconds in buckets filled with frigid, 57-degree water. (Keep in mind that 57-degree water feels much colder than 57-degree air.)

The second trial was similar, except that they kept their hands submerged for 90 seconds instead of 60, and during the final 30 seconds, the water warmed up to 59 degrees. That final half minute was still unpleasant, but noticeably less so for most participants. (Note the researchers were monitoring the time carefully, but the participants were not told how much time had elapsed.)

For the third painful experience, the participants were given a choice: Would you rather repeat the first trial or the second?

This is an easy question: Both trials featured 60 seconds of identical pain, and the second trial added another 30 seconds of slightly reduced pain. So, this is kind of like asking, would you rather be slapped in the face for 60 seconds or 90 seconds? Nevertheless, 69% chose the longer trial.

Psychologists have untangled the reasons for this puzzling result. When people assess and experience, they tend to forget or ignore its length – a phenomenon called "duration neglect." Instead, they seem to rate the experience based on two key moments: (1) the best or worst moment, known as the "peak"; and (2) the ending. Psychologists call it the "peak-end rule."

So, in the participants' memories, the difference between the 60 and 90 seconds washed out. That's duration neglect. And what stood out for them was that the longer trial ended more comfortably than the short one. (Both trials, by the way, had a similar peak moment of pain.)

What's indisputable is that when we assess our experiences, we don't average our minute-by-minute sensations. Rather, we tend to remember flagship moments: the peaks, the pits, and the transitions."[1]

The 244-mile hike which led us to crest 12 mountains proved to be very difficult, but also naturally provided a lot of peaks, pits, and transitional moments. The ending of the hike gave the seven of us an exhilaration lasting several days. The peak moments along with the satisfying feeling of accomplishment and pride felt with completing the hike, calls us all back to the mountain. I wonder if this is what John Muir was speaking of when he said, *"The Mountains are calling, and I must go."*

The peak moments for me may not be what you are thinking. The summit of Mt. Whitney was a moment I will never forget. The views from passes we would hike

[1] Chip Heath and Dan Heath, *The Power of Moments: Why Certain Experiences have Extraordinary Impact* (New York : Simon & Schuster, 2017), 8–9.

through were indescribable at times. The stars at night left us all in awe of God's creation. I could go on and on about the memories and peak moments. However, I also experienced unforgettable moments of prayer. Prayer provides power.

> On a mountainside in Galilee, Jesus taught his first sermon, a sermon about the coming of the Kingdom of God. It was there on the mountain that he introduced the disciples and surrounding crowd to a perspective of God, a groundbreaking revelation.[2]

I once posed the following request on Facebook. *Please answer the following question with a one-word answer. "Prayer is ..."* I received over 60 different responses. Let me share them with you. The top three responses were given nine, six, and five times. Those one-word top three answers were: Powerful, Communication and Essential. Let me list for you the other responses. I don't believe any of them are wrong.

> Life-Line, Connecting, Powerful, Conversation, Required, Personal, Intimate, Vital, Essential, Sustaining, Everything, Hope, Important, Need-

[2] Jarrett Stephens, *The Mountains are Calling: Making the Climb for a Clearer View of God and Ourselves* (Colorado Springs: Multnomah, 2018), 88.

ed, Comforting, Reliable, Refreshing, Faith, Forgiveness Awesome, Humbling, Simple, Appeal, Life, Communion, Submission, Healing, Life-changing, Worship, Trust, Love, Relationship, Rewarding, Peace, Privilege, Must, Bonding, Answers, Syncing-up, Calming, Communication, Constant, Enlightening, Effective, Transcendent, Amazing, Necessary, Relief, Access, Rest, Wise, Thanksgiving, Obedience, Breath, Good, Completion, Neglected, Reassurance, Peace, Change

I must confess I have never considered myself a person of prayer. I want to get better at it, and I want to pray more powerfully and passionately. I, like the disciples on top of Mt. Eremos, want to learn to pray. Adam Clarke says, *"Prayer requires more of the heart than the tongue."*[3] Guy King says, *"No one is a firmer believer in the power of prayer than the devil, not that he practices it, but he suffers from it."*[4] Let's look at the model prayer Jesus gave the disciple on top of the mountain.

Matthew 6:9–13, Pray then like this: "Our Father in heaven, hallowed be your name. Your kingdom come, your will be done, on earth as it is in heaven. Give us this day our daily bread, and

[3] Adam Clarke, *Christian Theology*, 252.

[4] King, Guy. Quotations *about Prayer,* The Quote Garden, www.quotegarden.com/prayer

forgive us our debts, as we also have forgiven our debtors. And lead us not into temptation but deliver us from evil.

Prayer is a conversation based on a relationship. Prayer produces power. Prayer leads us into the presence of God. I want to use the rest of this chapter to explain the basics of prayer. The goal in this chapter is to ask and answer the two questions: Who do we pray to? Who can pray?

1. Who do We Pray to?

A. We Pray to God the Father.

Matthew 6:5–9, And when you pray, you must not be like the hypocrites. For they love to stand and pray in the synagogues and at the street corners, that they may be seen by others. Truly, I say to you, they have received their reward. But when you pray, go into your room and shut the door and pray to your Father who is in secret. And your Father who sees in secret will reward you. "And when you pray, do not heap up empty phrases as the Gentiles do, for they think that they will be heard for their many words. Do not be like them, for your Father knows what you need before you ask him. Pray then like this: "Our Father in heaven, hallowed be your name.

In these few verses, Jesus says, "Father" four times. He is teaching the disciples to pray to God the Father. Father in Aramaic is the word, *Abba*, which means, 'Daddy.' 17 times in this sermon, Jesus used this word to describe God. It's used only nine times in all the Old Testament. Jesus was making a strong point regarding the relationship God has with those in His family. The Lord God has many names, but this one seems to carry with it an extra amount of tenderness and affection. Here are a few of the names of God and their definitions.

Jehovah JIREH	The Lord My Provider
Genesis 22:14	
Jehovah RAPHA	The Lord Who Heals
Exodus 15:26	
Jehovah NISSI	The Lord My Banner
Exodus 17:15–16	
Jehovah MAKADESH	The Lord Who Sanctifies
Leviticus 20:7–18	
Jehovah SHALOM	The Lord My Peace
Judges 6:24	
Jehovah ROHI	The Lord My Shepherd
Psalm 23:1	
Jehovah SHAMMAH	The Lord Who is Present
Ezekiel 48:35	

Jesus tells the disciples and us to talk to God the Father as we would talk to our own Dad. The picture is also of a dad listening attentively to his child. Process those two sentences. We can approach God the Father as a caring, loving, compassionate daddy. Picture a small child tugging at their daddy's pant leg as he stops everything, bends down, and listens. God longs to hear from His children. Remember, prayer is a conversation based on a relationship and prayer provides power.

B. We Pray to God the Father through God the Son.

John 14:6, Jesus said to him, "I am the way, and the truth, and the life. No one comes to the Father except through me.

John 14:13–14, Whatever you ask in my name, this I will do, that the Father may be glorified in the Son. If you ask me anything in my name, I will do it.

Hebrews 4:14–16, Since then we have a great high priest who has passed through the heavens, Jesus, the Son of God, let us hold fast our confession. For we do not have a high priest who is unable to sympathize with our weaknesses, but one who in every respect has been tempted as we are, yet without sin. Let us then with confidence draw near to the throne of grace, that we may receive mercy and find grace to help in time of need.

Jesus' death tore down the wall of separation between man and God. All who have placed their faith in Jesus have direct access to God the Father through God the Son. Jesus gives us an all access pass to God the Father, Abba, Dad.

C. We Pray to God the Father, through God the Son, Empowered by the Holy Spirit.

> **Ephesians 6:18,** praying at all times in the Spirit, with all prayer and supplication. To that end keep alert with all perseverance, making supplication for all the saints.
> **Jude 1:20,** But you, beloved, building yourselves up in your most holy faith and praying in the Holy Spirit.

The first question we asked and now answered is, "Who do we pray to?" Prayer is a conversation based on a relationship. We pray to God the Father, through God the son, empowered by the Holy Spirit, but "Who can pray?"

D. Who Can Pray to God the Father?

"Jesus brought a change of perspective on the mountain. He taught the people that they had access to God and could connect to him as an earthly child would connect to his earthly father."[5]

Prayer is a conversation based on a relationship. The relationship between child and Father in which Jesus talks about is personal, loving, and eternal. Let me take a moment to further unpack these thoughts.

E. Prayer is a Conversation Based on a Personal Relationship.

John 1:9–12, The true light, which gives light to everyone, was coming into the world. [10] He was in the world, and the world was made through him, yet the world did not know him. He came to his own, and his own people did not receive him. *But to all who did receive him,* who believed in his name, he gave the right to become children of God.

Ephesians 1:3–6, Blessed be the God and Father of our Lord Jesus Christ, who has blessed us in Christ with every spiritual blessing in the heavenly places, even as he chose us in him before the foundation of the world, that we should be holy and blameless before him. In love *he predestined us for adoption as sons through Jesus Christ,* according to the purpose of his will, to the praise of

[5] Stephens, *The Mountains are Calling*, 93.

his glorious grace, with which he has blessed us in the Beloved.

Romans 8:15–17, For you did not receive the spirit of slavery to fall back into fear, but you have received the Spirit of adoption as sons, by whom we cry, "Abba! Father!" The Spirit himself bears witness with our spirit that we are children of God, and if children, then heirs—heirs of God and fellow heirs with Christ, provided we suffer with him in order that we may also be glorified with him.

Please don't read too fast. Take a moment to process what you have read. Prayer is communication with God the Father based on a personal relationship. Psalm 23 is one of the most quoted passages of scripture. The Psalmist says, The Lord is MY shepherd I shall not want. The relationship we can have with God is personal. He is a personal God who has chosen to reveal Himself through His Son. We have access to communicate to God, because of His Son. WOW! What an amazing gift.

F. Prayer is a Conversation Based on a Loving Relationship.

Romans 8:35–39, Who shall separate us from the love of Christ? Shall tribulation, or distress, or persecution, or famine, or nakedness, or danger, or sword? As it is written, "For your sake we are being killed all the day long; we are regarded as sheep to be slaughtered." No, in all these things we are more than conquerors through him who loved us. For I am sure that neither death nor life, nor angels nor rulers, nor things present nor things to come, nor powers, nor height nor depth, nor anything else in all creation, will be able to separate us from the love of God in Christ Jesus our Lord.

John 3:16, "For God so loved the world, that he gave his only Son, that whoever believes in him should not perish but have eternal life.

1 John 4:10, In this is love, not that we have loved God but that he loved us and sent his Son to be the propitiation for our sins.

God loved you so much He sent His son to die in your place. Jesus willingly laid down His life because of His love for you. He died so you could live. He died so you can pray directly to God. John Stott said, *"Until you see the cross as that which is done by you, you will never appreciate that it is done for you."*[6]

---

[6] John Stott, The Cross of Christ (Downers Grove: IVP, 1986).

Romans 5:8, but God shows his love for us in that while we were still sinners, Christ died for us.

G. Prayer is a Conversation Based on an Eternal Relationship.

1 John 5:12–13, Whoever has the Son has life; whoever does not have the Son of God does not have life. I write these things to you who believe in the name of the Son of God that you may know that you have eternal life.

Ephesians 1:13–14, In him you also, when you heard the word of truth, the gospel of your salvation, and believed in him, were sealed with the promised Holy Spirit, who is the guarantee of our inheritance until we acquire possession of it, to the praise of his glory.

Prayer is a privilege of children of God The option to be a child of God is yours to make. God sent his son Jesus to die in your place so you could have a personal, loving, and eternal relationship with God. All you need to do is confess your faith in Jesus. Confess He is Lord. Confess Jesus is the only way to God and turn from your sin and yourself and turn to JESUS. The privilege of the child of

God is open dialogue with God the Father, through God the Son; empowered by the Holy Spirit.

The hike brought some interesting peak moments I will never forget. They make the thought of attempting the JMT seem possible and even pleasant. I remember the first night we camped. We were anxious about what the first day of hiking would entail. I was excited, nervous, and emotional. Aaron, my brother-in-law, and I walked up a little hill that overlooked our campsite. We had an uplifting time of prayer, asking God to reveal himself to us as we began this remarkable adventure. This was a peak moment for me, and I imagine, for Aaron as well.

Day after day, we forced ourselves out of our warm sleeping bag to experience the cold mountain morning. One morning, I remember waking up to near freezing dew dropping from the roof of my tent onto my face. Getting out of the warm sleeping bag was one of the first and biggest accomplishments every morning. The team would gather up most mornings and pray. Joey would read the verse of the day before we prayed, and then the morning hike would begin. As I reflect, the memory of team prayer was a peak moment for me.

The private conversations I had with the Lord in my tent many nights were personal and fervent. I do not believe I have ever prayed with such passion and persistence as I did on the hike. The power I found in prayer literally got me up each morning and up the mountains each day. I honestly believe the only way I was able to complete the hike was the power of prayer. I personally prayed like never before and many people were praying for me. I give God complete credit for getting me through. Multiple times on the trip I had considered getting off the trail and quitting. The first time this became a consideration was on day two. Sickness was already a problem for me, and yet summiting Mt. Whitney was supposed to happen on day three. The word got around camp that two people who were planning on hiking the entire 17 days, had made the decision to exit early on day five with the rest of the team. The van would be too full for me to exit early, so the prospect of leaving on day five was no longer an option.

Prayer provides power. The inability to eat led me to be extremely weak, tired and exhausted. Many nights, while lying in my tent, I begged God to allow me to be able to eat and sleep so I could have energy needed for each day. I knew the only way for me to complete this hike would be through God's power. Breathing while carrying a 35 lb. pack, climbing a 2,000-foot pass at over 12,000 feet of elevation, while lacking proper nutrition, proved to be very difficult. Early in the hike, focusing on my breathing became essential. Years ago, I learned while jogging, two breaths in through my nose and one large exhale out of my mouth worked best. This did not prove to work well while climbing. I learned longer deeper breaths worked to my advantage. I knew God would have to empower me to get up the mountain, and yet I didn't have the energy or the breath to pray. God gave me a way to do both. Slowing my breathing down and taking long, deep breaths allowed me to keep going. I decided the way I would talk with God while climbing, would be to call his name as I took each breath. Let me see if I can explain and have you experience as you read. Inhale a long, deep, slow breath through your nose. Ready. Go. I'll wait.

Don't forget to let it out!

Exhale slowly through your mouth. Repeat this pattern, inhale slowly through your nose and exhale slowly through your mouth. Continue this pattern three consecutive times. I created a pattern using this format of breathing in a repeated cycle three times. Each time I inhaled and exhaled it would be in this three-pattern cycle. I would talk to God. Here is what I would say. It is not profound, but it was powerful.

1. God the Father
2. God the Son
3. God the Spirit

As I inhaled, I would say, "God the Father", and then exhale. Then I would inhale again and say, "God the Son" and then exhale. In the final round of this cycle, I would say, "God the Spirit" as I inhaled and then slowly exhaled. The switchbacks which crossed back and forth and back and forth were mind numbing. However, in the struggle of the climb, I learned prayer leads to power. Prayer is a conversation based on a relationship. We pray to God the Father, through God the son, empowered by God the Spirit. I prayed my way up the mountain and the prayer leading to power has proved to be a peak, leading me to say once again, *I MUST GO!*

CHAPTER 7—IDENTITY IN HIM

Jon's Tale from the Trail

No one wants to be "THAT GUY". You know who I am talking about. No one wants to be the person who _____. You can fill in the blank. What we are known for and how we are known seems to drive us individually and as a culture. This infatuation of who we are and what people think of us fuels social media. Remember the old Sprite campaign? *"Image is nothing. Thirst is everything. Obey your thirst."* I believe this advertisement came out in the late 1990's. I am not sure this ad could be any more wrong in our current culture. However, they were using famous sports stars to convey their message. The message was counterintuitive to what they were trying to convey.

The hike revealed some truth about who I am and my opinion of myself. Days on the trail, in which I didn't think I could make it, afforded me a lot of time to reflect on who I am and what I think about myself. My brother and I are very competitive and what people think of us as individuals is a powerful motivator. I am the older twin, by a whopping six minutes. The dynamic of being the older twin is weird. You can google tons of information regarding birth order and how your birth order impacts your personality. The psychology behind that is interesting. I was the middle child until I was twelve, but I was also the older twin. When I was twelve years old, we welcomed a new sister into our house. We had adopted a little baby girl. My brother and I were now both in the middle, having an older and younger sister. My brother was no longer the baby. I was no longer in the middle. However, I was still the oldest twin. WOW! As I type this, I feel confused. "WHO AM I?" Maybe I need counseling. I have taken a side hike from where this was headed. Let me get back on the trail. See what I did there?

The hike brought out the best and the worst of me. My fear of failure leads me to extreme behavior sometimes. The distress of letting people down leads me to live for others and their approval too often. I remember having this inner battle in my mind one day as I hiked alone for miles while being filled with fear and anxiety. What if I don't finish? What will people think if I cannot make it? I don't want to be that guy! I remember when I got back hearing my son and my father-in-law stating they knew I would not leave the trail early, especially since my brother was on the trail. They knew I would have to be taken off because of my uber competitive spirit. Add in the fact I am ultra-stubborn, and you have a recipe for someone who would have to be drug off the mountain. This is a good thing. Or is it?

Do I find my identity in my accomplishments or who I am in Christ? Honestly, most of the time it is in my accomplishments. These thoughts are rooted in pride, not Christ. Jesus resists the proud and gives grace to the humble. I feel an inner struggle even now as I type this. I find my identity in who I am more often than in WHOSE I am. Do you find your identity in Christ or in yourself?

Michael's Tale from the Trail

While on the trail, many people are given trail names. One day we met a lady who had given herself the name, "The woman who sings." She joyfully serenaded everyone she met. As far as I know, I was not given a trail name, but who knows what I might have been called behind my back. Some of the names given to the guys in our group were as follows. Joey was given several names, but the main one was "Keto", which was explained earlier. Austin Crow (pp. 198–199), the only single guy on the trip, was given the name "Brown Sugar." It was day 11, and our spirits were at an all-time high thanks to our night spent at MTR. We had eaten an incredible breakfast that morning and were also able to pack a sack lunch which included fresh deli meat. At this point of the hike, we had settled into a pretty good daily routine, which allowed us to enjoy the hike and our time together a little more. Seldon Pass awaited us, but we all stopped for lunch so we could enjoy these amazing sandwiches. While sitting on a log and taking in the sun, a couple of ladies from Oklahoma stopped to share stories from their trip. Austin said, "Hey, you want some brown sugar (awkward pause) pop-tarts"? I know this story will fall immensely short from being as funny to you, as it was, and remains to be to us. Andrew, who did all the work to put this hike together, was given the name, "Mountain Goat." I don't know what all he did to get physically ready for this hike, but any time we came to a big climb, he left us tasting the dust he left behind. Darrell Ibach, aka "Butch" (pp. 200–202), was given the name "Bonfire." We all had envisioned a leisurely campfire every night of the hike, but we quickly learned those ideas were only fairytales. Several nights, towards the end of our journey, we did get to enjoy a campfire. Butch was our man. Butch loved to make us a fire and his motto was, "the bigger the better." Lonnie could be seen fueling the fire by carrying back trees to keep it going. When I say trees, I literally mean trees. Lonnie didn't really have a trail name, although there are many we could choose from. Names like: "Shirtless", "The Man who Sings", "Tentless" or "Encourager." I have looked up to Lonnie since I was in high school. He is a guy, like Butch, who has never met a stranger. This would prove valuable at a specific point on our hike. The day Andrew and Lonnie went back to find Shawn was an extremely long day for them. Somewhere on that hike, Lonnie sat down to take a break. When he got up to get back on the trail, he failed to realize his tent was no longer attached to his backpack. He tried to sleep under the stars that night. We were camped out close to a lake and the next morning we woke up with condensation soaking everything. Needless to say, he was wet and cold. The next night, he used my hammock and he felt like he was meat, hanging for a bear to come enjoy. While eating lunch at Reds Meadow, Lonnie struck up a conversation with our waitress. She was not in a great mood because it was Labor Day, which is their busiest day of the year. On top of that, they were short-staffed. Being an encourager and always looking for a chance to share the story of MANNA, this was a challenge to him. Eventually, the lady sat down with us and her attitude had done a complete one-eighty. It was through this conversation, we would meet up with this waitress the next morning, and Lonnie purchased a hiking tent from her. God provided a tent, simply because Lonnie was willing to talk to an overworked, underpaid waitress. One of the things we struggle with when it comes to our identity is, we focus way too much on what others think about us. While it is honorable to live a life, which causes people to speak favorably about you, this is not the goal. The goal is not to please man. The goal is to point people to Him. Live your life in the light of who He is and who He created you to be. This will allow the gifts God placed inside of you to shine brightly. No matter what others call you, remember you are loved.

Mount Hermon

Our culture has an infatuation with identity. We all wrestle with who or what people think about us. Did you know that this is not a new phenomenon? Jesus himself asked the disciples a question regarding who people said He was. Why would Jesus ask this question? His family accused Him of being crazy. "He is out of His mind," is what we are told in Mark 3:21. Jesus was accused of doing the work of Satan as one of his demons. The religious elite exclaimed He was speaking heresy. Nicodemus was one of those pious select, but he wanted to know the truth of the identity of Jesus. Covered by the darkness of night, he came to Him and asked Him who He was and from where He had come. From the poor in need of a physician, to the palace full of power, the world had the same question; "Who is this man?" Let's eavesdrop on the conversation which took place between Jesus and His disciples just before He took them to the mountain where He would unveil His identity.

Luke 9:18–20, Now it happened that as He was praying alone, the disciples were with him. And He asked them, "Who do the crowds say that I am?" And they answered, "John the Baptist. But others say, Elijah, and others, that one of the

prophets of old has risen." Then He said to them,
"But who do you say that I am?" And Peter answered, "The Christ of God."

In Matthew's gospel, Jesus affirms Peter's account.
Jesus goes on to tell him it is on this truth; He would build
His church. Why was there so much misunderstanding as
to the identity of Jesus? The prophet Isaiah gives us a hint
why there was so much uncertainty concerning the identity of this man from Nazareth. "He had no form or majesty
that we should look at Him, and no beauty that we should
desire Him" (Isaiah 53:2). Jesus taught with authority and
had performed a few miracles, but aside from these moments, He was just an ordinary man.

Jesus would take them from this garden moment to a
life-altering experience on the mountain. Jesus was going
to unveil His identity to His inner circle. He was going to
show them who He was, as opposed to just speaking of
who He was. Remember, mountaintop moments are for us
to be informed of who He is and then to inspire us to share
what we have learned with the world.

Matthew 17:1–8, And after six days Jesus took
with him Peter and James, and John his brother,
and led them up a high mountain by themselves.
And he was transfigured before them, and his face

shone like the sun, and his clothes became white as light. And behold, there appeared to them Moses and Elijah, talking with him. And Peter said to Jesus, "Lord, it is good that we are here. If you wish, I will make three tents here, one for you and one for Moses and one for Elijah." He was still speaking when, behold, a bright cloud overshadowed them, and a voice from the cloud said, "This is my beloved Son, with whom I am well pleased; listen to him." When the disciples heard this, they fell on their faces and were terrified. But Jesus came and touched them, saying, "Rise, and have no fear." And when they lifted up their eyes, they saw no one but Jesus only.

Jesus ascended the mountain with Peter, James and John so He could reveal his identity for one glorious moment. While Jesus walked this earth in physical form, His Deity had been veiled in humility. On Mount Hermon, the physical reality would make room for the spiritual reality of who Jesus was and break into the world of man for the first time. Our English word, "metamorphosis" is taken from the Greek word used here. On a much smaller scale, we can compare this metamorphosis to a caterpillar morphing into a butterfly.

Two important truths we can learn from the transfigu-
ration is Jesus has no rival and He is the only one worthy
of our worship. While Moses represents the law and Elijah
represents the prophets, Jesus came to fulfill them both.
Immediately, Peter wanted to set up tents so they could all
be worshipped, but God quickly shows Peter only Jesus
is worthy of our worship. While the three disciples fell in
fear, Jesus was left standing alone. One commentator says,
*"The primary purpose of Moses and Elijah was to salute
their divine Successor, and then to leave Him alone in His
unchallenged supremacy, the sole object of His disciples'
veneration."*[1]

I believe the root of our identity issues is we fail to
really see Jesus for who He is. When we truly see Jesus,
it will lead us to seek only Him. We will search for Him
above all and worship Him alone. Seeing or connecting
with Jesus and growing in our understanding of Him, is
vital to our growth in who we are. You might not remember when the internet first started making a splash around
the world, but I sure do. AOL cd's were at the counter of
every store. I was living in Pueblo, Colorado at the time
and only a few numbers could connect you to the World
Wide Web. You would hear the dial-up noise and the following noise probably still causes night sweats for many.

[1] R.V.G. Tasker, *Matthew*, Tyndale New Testament Commentaries
(Grand Rapids: Eerdmans, 1961) 164–65.

It could take hours to get online and once you got on, it could take hours to upload or download anything. What is keeping you from ascending the mountain to see Jesus clearly? What is it that is hindering your connection? What is keeping you from seeing yourself the way Jesus sees you? Maybe you are guilty of spending most of your time hearing what others say about who He is instead of going to the mountain to see for yourself. We live in a wonderful time in history, because we can listen to powerful preachers, inspirational podcasts and uplifting music from all over the world. I think all of these are needed, but if we aren't careful, we can be guilty of only seeing Jesus through the lenses of others. Go to His Word and listen to Him. Go to your closet and speak to Him.

> Have you ever wondered how best to spend your time as a Christian? Well, we all know that there is no substitute for seeking the Lord with your whole heart, but why does it so often feel like such a chore? Imagine walking up a mountain alone. But it's no ordinary mountain. The ground beneath you is shaking, and the entire mountain is covered in smoke. At its peak is a thick cloud with lightning and thunder. God descends onto the mountain in fire, and each time you speak to

him, he responds in thunder. This is what Moses experienced in Exodus 19.[2]

Jesus radiated the glory of God, while Moses reflected the glory of God. We will never truly reflect the glory of the Son, like the moon reflects the sun, unless we come near and connect with Him. The more we lean into Him, the less we will listen to the voices of this world.

Take a few minutes to read these verses and allow His Word to speak to you and remind you of who you are in Christ.

Jeremiah 1:5, Before I formed you in the womb, I knew you, and before you were born I consecrated you; I appointed you a prophet to the nations.

1 Peter 1:9, But you are a chosen race, a royal priesthood, a holy nation, a people for his own possession, that you may proclaim the excellencies of him who called you out of darkness into his marvelous light.

1 Corinthians 6:19–20, Or do you not know that your body is a temple of the Holy Spirit within you, whom you have from God? You are not your own, for you were bought with a price. So glorify God in your body."

[2] Francis Chan, "The Greatest Thing You Could Do." www.desiringgod.org/articles.

Colossians 3:1–3, If then you have been raised with Christ, seek the things that are above, where Christ is, seated at the right hand of God. Set your minds on things that are above, not on things that are on earth. For you have died, and your life is hidden with Christ in God.

Ephesians 2:10, For we are his workmanship, created in Christ Jesus for good works, which God prepared beforehand, that we should walk in them.

I want us to spend the rest of this chapter on the promise we see here in Ephesians. Workmanship literally means, "A thing of His making;" "handiwork." Your life is a masterpiece and God has uniquely designed you for a divine purpose. The first book I wrote is entitled, *Positioning your Life for A Breakthrough*. One of my biggest fears when it was being published, was somehow it was going to be printed as it was before the editor got a hold of it. A book published with my picture on it, with tons of mistakes caused me to lose sleep at night. While waiting on my first two-hundred and fifty books, other people had ordered some and received them. This only enhanced my fear. I finally ordered one on Amazon Prime, so I could see it for myself and hopefully put my mind at ease. Late one night, I got a message on Instagram from a friend of mine who is a missionary in Mongolia. He said he had bought my book on Kindle and was enjoying it. He also went on to say, "I think I got the editor's edition." Immediately, I was wide awake. My seemingly irrational fear was now a rational reality. Somehow, Chris had been given the Kindle version containing every red mark and every suggested edit given for this book. No one wants people to see their unfinished project. The closer we get to God, the more we understand we are a story He is still writing. Hopefully, this knowledge will allow us to extend more grace to other Christians still receiving the application of God's brushstrokes. We spend too much time comparing our story with someone else's story when we have no clue what chapter their life is on right now. Comparison will either puff you up with pride or deflate you with depression. Your identity is in Christ, and the closer you get to Him the easier that is to believe and live out. Our trail names while we are here on earth should simply be, "Masterpiece." When we acknowledge God is still in the process of sanctifying us, it is much easier when He calls us to the mountain to see Him and say, *I MUST GO*!

CHAPTER 8—HOPE IN THE HURT

Michael's Tale from the Trail

Labor Day had us looking at a 19-mile trek ahead of us, but we were excited to get to Reds Meadow for a juicy cheeseburger and a Dr. Pepper. As we walked into civilization, we were overcome with how many tourists we saw. We would find out later this is their busiest day of the year. All these lovely families had been bussed out here so they could take a short hike to see Devil's Post-Pile National Monument. It was one of the few moments in my life I felt like people feared me. These poor families seemed to be hiding their kids from this group of hikers who looked like they were on a death march.

We waited around for a while trying to figure out if there was a place to stay and if so, how we could get there. The line for the public transportation was excruciatingly long. Butch came through and found a condo for us to sleep in for the night. He also managed to get a taxi company to come out and pick us up. The condo was phenomenal. We ordered some pizza and enjoyed our time in the hot tub.

This was also the first time on the trip we were able to do laundry in an actual washing machine. The water in that washing machine was horribly filthy after running 13-day-old dirty clothes through them.

I'm not sure why my feet were swollen so badly that night, but I was having a hard time walking. Lying on the floor, I spent some time in prayer for the swelling in my feet to subside. The pizza, hot tub, shower and laundry were all wonderful, but nothing compared to getting to talk to my family. Hurting and tired, it was refreshing and encouraging to know they were cheering for me. Thankfully, I woke up the next morning and my feet were back to normal. Unfortunately, the blisters were all still there, but at least my feet could fit into my shoes. It is amazing what hope can do for you. Each day one of us was struggling with something. Many times, it was a small thing which provided us enough hope to keep going. Such encouragements could be our re-supply on day five, day ten hot springs and shower, cheeseburger at Reds Meadows or another hot meal in Tuolumne Meadows. The box of Hot Tamales my wife surprised me with in my last resupply was simple, but sensational. Hope amid your pain is potent.

Jon's Tale from the Trail

Day six was an interesting day. I had not been feeling well, but the morning "walk" was one of my favorites. We had a beautiful seven-mile gradual downhill hike. I took this morning to be alone. I put my headphones on, listened to worship music and enjoyed an amazing time talking out loud to God. I even listened a few hours to an audible book. Everyone gathered that day for lunch at the famous suspension bridge. I was taking my time eating my lunch and feeling pretty good after a long walk-through, stunning, plush green forest. I suddenly realized everyone had begun the long climb up and I was by myself. I felt a little panicked but packed my things while trying to dry them out and began the afternoon hike. I, like everyone else, took video of the walk across the wobbly bridge suspended over the fast-moving melted snow through this beautiful canyon. The video documents me admitting it was much scarier than anticipated. The afternoon climb proved to be much more taxing than any of us had calculated. We were going to climb nearly 3,000 feet over a seven-mile stretch. The trail was beautiful and paralleled the rushing water which could be heard for miles. I passed Shawn as he was taking a breather just on the other side of the bridge. Butch was the next person I would come across. Butch was concerned for Shawn, so we took frequent breaks to make sure he was coming behind us. A few miles up the mountain, while overlooking the huge opening of the water rushing down the mountain, we had a million-dollar view while waiting for our lone hiker to catch us. Shawn (181-186) suddenly appeared and was a little emotional. He was praising God for giving him a miracle. "What miracle", we asked? The reason he was stopped just beyond the suspension bridge was to pause and pray. He was hurting and he decided to take a moment with God. He let us know although his pace was not as fast as he would have liked it, he had not stopped the entire few miles of climbing. He felt God had given him the air in his lungs and the strength in his legs. He felt a nearness to God over the past few miles, he was struggling to describe.

Shawn's father was his inspiration to tackle this monumental hike of a lifetime. Shawn's father was an avid outdoorsman who had hiked the entire Appalachian trail by himself, after he retired. The Appalachian Trail is approximately 2,200 miles and extends from Springer Mountain, Georgia to Mount Katahdin in Maine. Shawn and Lonnie used a lot of Jerry's gear to honor his memory. Jerry, Shawn's father, had passed away and this was an opportunity for Shawn to reconnect with the Lord, the outdoors, and his father. The three of us had an unforgettable time of prayer half-way up the mountain that day. We thanked God for the closeness we felt to the Lord, Jerry, and each other. Shawn was emotional. All three of us were emotional. The hurt felt that day was not from the mountain, but from the heart. God allowed this moment of healing and hope to burst through the hurt. I am thankful while even in our hurt, God gives hope.

Mount Olivet

"More often than not, when we think about mountain top moments or experiences, we think positive thoughts. We don't think about the tough times, the trials we go through. We consider these the valleys, the low times in life. Those dark and lonely times, though, can bring us to a fuller understanding of God, a richer experience of him. They can be their own sort of midnight mountain top experience."[1]

Jesus had such a moment on top of a mountain. Jesus and his disciples celebrated Passover the night he would be arrested. Jesus led them from the Passover meal to the Mt. of Olives. This mountaintop is where he would pray in the Garden of Gethsemane. Recently, my wife and I were blessed to go to Israel. Our trip overflowed with many moments of passion, prayer, and sensing the presence and closeness of God. Joy and I sat in the structure, built on the Mt. of Olives in the midst of the Garden. The feeling of God's presence was tangible. We prayed about the anguish Jesus felt in this exact spot over 2000 years ago. The hurt, heartache, and pain Jesus felt that night as He poured out his soul to His father, is beyond my comprehension.

[1] Jarrett Stephens, *The Mountains are Calling: Making the Climb for a Clearer View of God and Ourselves* (Colorado Springs: Multnomah, 2018), 117.

Literally, the weight and sin of the world were placed on His shoulders.

> **Mark 14:32–34,** Then they came to a place which was named Gethsemane; and He said to His disciples, "Sit here while I pray." And He took Peter, James, and John with Him, and He began to be troubled and deeply distressed. Then He said to them, "My soul is exceedingly sorrowful, *even* to death. Stay here and watch."

My wife and I sat on top of the Mt. of Olives and prayed. We were in the very place in which Jesus, my Lord and Savior, wept and felt His deepest emotional pain. His hurt and suffering are beyond what any of us could imagine. Joy and I were overwhelmed with a heaviness difficult to put into words. Our hearts hurt as we thought about how much Jesus' heart hurt. Why did Jesus do this? Why did Jesus choose to go to the cross?

> **Hebrews 12:1–2,** Therefore, since we are surrounded by so great a cloud of witnesses, let us also lay aside every weight, and sin which clings so closely, and let us run with endurance the race that is set before us, looking to Jesus, the founder and perfecter of our faith, who for the joy that was set before him endured the cross, despising

the shame, and is seated at the right hand of the throne of God.

Our Lord endured far more than did any of the heroes of faith named in Hebrews 11, and therefore He is a perfect example for us to follow. He endured the cross! This involved shame, suffering, the "contradiction [opposition]" of sinners, and even temporary rejection by the Father. On the cross He suffered for all the sins of all the world! Yet He endured and finished the work the Father gave Him to do (John 17:4). What was it that enabled our Lord to endure the cross? It was our Lord's faith that enabled Him to endure. He kept the eye of faith on "the joy that was set before Him." "the joy that was set before Him" would include Jesus' completing the Father's will, His resurrection and exaltation, and His joy in presenting believers to the Father in glory (Jude 24). Throughout this epistle, the writer emphasized the importance of the future hope. His readers were prone to look back and want to go back, but he encouraged them to follow Christ's example and look ahead by faith.[2]

---

[2] Waren W. Wiersbe, *Bible Exposition Commentary (BE Series): New Testament*, Volume 2 (Wheaton: Victor, 1989).

Jesus bravely looked to the cross and His suffering with His eyes on you and me. The joy set before him was presenting His bride, the church, to His Father. His hope in his hurt was rescuing me and you. WOW! Bask in the truth of that reality. Jesus was in anguish of spirit and yet, He was thinking of you. He was about to be arrested, beaten, and hung on a tree, yet his hope was the joy of rescuing me.

This picture of Jesus suffering in the garden screams in the face of those who say, "All your problems will go away if you put your trust in Jesus." I am typing this on March 15, 2020. Today's events were a first-time experience for me. As you read this, I pray this day will be looked back on as a huge overreaction. Many churches did not meet in their buildings today. Many churches live streamed their services, due to the Coronavirus (COVID-19). The mayor of Ft. Worth, where I live, set a directive requiring all gatherings of more than 250 people be cancelled. Therefore, I preached from my back porch this morning, while our church members joined via Facebook from all over the Metroplex. My phone is blowing up currently from a text message group of pastor friends. The CDC has just recommended no gatherings of more than 50 people take place for the next eight weeks. I feel my heart rate being elevated and my blood pressure rising. What are we going to do? What is the next step? These are the first of many questions flooding my mind and the thoughts of every other pastor I know. How can we, like Jesus, hope in the hurt?

Here is a novel idea. Do what Jesus did. *"Jesus modeled the truths of suffering, but he also modeled exactly what we should do when trying times come our way."*[3] He prayed. Jesus took time to have a conversation with his Father. The transparency Jesus reveals through His prayer is astounding.

> **Mark 14:32–39,** And they went to a place called Gethsemane. And he said to his disciples, "Sit here while I pray." And he took with him Peter and James and John and began to be greatly distressed and troubled. And he said to them, "My soul is very sorrowful, even to death. Remain here and watch." And going a little farther, he fell on the ground and prayed that, if it were possible, the hour might pass from him. And he said, "Abba, Father, all things are possible for you. Remove this cup from me. Yet not what I will, but what you will." And he came and found them sleeping, and he said to Peter, "Simon, are you asleep? Could you not watch one hour? Watch and pray that you may not enter into temptation.

[3] Stephens, *The Mountains are Calling*, 128.

The spirit indeed is willing, but the flesh is weak."
And again he went away and prayed, saying the
same words.

"There was no pretense, just honesty and
transparency, suffering has a way of stripping us
of the façade we sometimes put in front of people
and leaving us bare before the Lord."[4]

Honesty in our prayer is powerful. The honesty in this
prayer of Jesus was significant and set a great example for
us. Yesterday, I preached the funeral of an amazing lady.
She was 79 years old and one of the most unassuming ladies you could ever meet. Many times, I visited her in the
hospital while her family surrounded her, and we were not
afforded private conversations. However, one day when
she was moved from ICU to palliative care, we had a private conversation. She was a little anxious about her emotions. She was ready to die. She undoubtedly knew she
had given her life to Jesus but was not excited about leaving this earth. In a moment of honesty and transparency,
she asked if it was wrong of her to not be more enthusiastic about departing this world. I took her to the Mt. of Olives and the prayer of Jesus in the garden. Jesus was fully
man and fully God as he wrestled with this same reality.
He cried out to God and gave us a look into His humanity

---

[4] Stephens, *The Mountains are Calling*, 128.

that day. She was comforted by the prayer of Jesus. Jesus not only prayed, but he also surrendered. He submitted to the will of the Father. He prayed with transparency and passion and asked the Father if there were any other way, he could rescue sinners. He finishes his prayer with a surrendered Spirit, *"nevertheless, not my will, but yours, be done."* Jesus wanted God the Father's plans to be accomplished, and if that means suffering, then so be it. Despite his hurt, he had hope. Hope in the future. Hope in the plan. Hope in the sinner who would be rescued because He endured the cross.

When the valley is low and the night is darkest, let's look to Jesus and model exactly how he responded to suffering rather than trying to avoid it. We pray. We surrender. We endure. In this, we will discover the nearness of God. Hope is a funny thing. Hope can keep someone on the mountain. I know it did for me. I sat in the little office at the place known as Muir Trail Ranch. I had not been able to eat a good meal in quite some time. I had no energy, and even less hope. I sat in this office charging my phone and planning my exit strategy. I learned this exact place was one of the easiest places to get off the trail. I was ready to be done. I was ready to feel well. I was ready to eat a meal without throwing up. MTR is in the middle of nowhere. However, I did learn I could walk an easy five miles, downhill, to a lake in the morning. I could then catch a ferry to a town where I could get a ride to an air-port. However, in a few hours I would be able to eat my first real meal in over ten days. I prayed God would allow me to eat that night and if He would allow me to eat, I would keep going. We sat down later to fresh homemade garlic bread, grilled vegetables and the entrée. The crown jewel of the night was the eggplant lasagna. If you ask any of the other men who ate the lasagna, they will rave about how good it tasted. Honestly, I don't remember tasting it. I forced myself to eat several pieces along with the bread and vegetables. I went to sleep that night worried and very prayerful. My prayer was simple," Please Lord, let me keep it down." I had made the decision if I was able to eat and not get sick, I would keep going. The ability to eat a meal gave me hope. Hal Lindsey said, "*Man can live about forty days without food, about three days without water, about eight minutes without air . . . but only for one second without hope.*"[5]

Psalm 34:17–19, When the righteous cry for help, the LORD hears and delivers them out of all their troubles. The LORD is near to the broken-hearted and saves the crushed in spirit. Many are the afflictions of the righteous, but the LORD delivers him out of them all.

---

[5] Hall Lindsey, www.goodreads.com/quotes.

When you are hurting remember hope can be found in Jesus. Take a page out of Jesus' playbook; pray, surrender, and endure. As you pray, remember the words of Jesus, "nevertheless not my will but your will be done." As you hope in the hurt, the Lord will allow you to say, *I MUST GO!*

CHAPTER 9—AGONY OF ABANDONMENT

Jon's Tale from the Trail

On days four and five, I spent much of my time alone. Shawn and Craig (181–191) had a much slower pace than I wanted to walk, and all the other guys had a much faster pace than I could maintain. Therefore, I spent a lot of time by myself. Hours alone, in fact. I don't do well alone. I allowed my mind to go to a dangerous place many times. I had cut my thumb at home a few days before we left. I thought it had healed up, but after a few days of carrying my trekking poles for eight hours a day, my cut opened again. I had cuts on several of my fingers. I was worried about them getting infected and tried to keep Leukotape on them. The tape never seemed to stay very well, and this only brought me more frustration and anxiety. Hours and hours alone climbing a mountain while extremely exhausted and lacking nutrition, was not providing a healthy mental environment for me.

Thankfully, Butch began to hang back with me on day six. Craig hiked out on day five, so this left Butch, Shawn, and me to bring up the tail most days. The day we hiked down the Golden Staircase, everyone decided to hike together. The day before had been an extremely long day, especially for Butch and Shawn. I am not sure what happened, but suddenly it was me and Shawn left behind. He stopped to eat, and I became very anxious about falling too far behind. The rest of our hike for the day was only about four or five miles, which ended up being one of the easiest days of the hike. Shawn appeared to be healthy. He was enjoying some shade, while sitting on a log, and preparing a big bottle of Gatorade. He had rolled his ankle earlier that morning. I gave him my ankle brace and asked him if he was ok and made sure he knew where we were meeting for camp that night. He assured me he was fine. His phone had died and needed to be charged for him to check his GPS and see the map of the trail. We looked on my phone to see the map and the spot on the trail where we had planned on stopping. I left him with my solar panel charger so he could charge his phone as he caught up with us. I caught the rest of the group as they had stopped just a half a mile up the trail to eat lunch. I felt relieved, but also knew Shawn was now by himself.

I would never see him on the trail again. He was Medevacked off the trail two days later via helicopter. You will hear his story later in the book. I felt guilt over leaving him on the trail. All of us did. We abandoned him. He does not see it that way and he has accepted my apology, but I felt we all had forsaken him. I was confident he was fine, as was he, but we should have never left him isolated.

Michael's Tale from the Trail

Excitement was welling up in my stomach as I traveled across the country. Joey, Butch and I were going to meet up at LAX before heading to a local church to take advantage of their missions' apartment. I had never met Butch before, and I quickly learned he has never met a stranger. Butch is the guy who talks at a louder decibel than most people, and he can definitely talk. Many times, we joked about how people on the trail could hear us way before they ever saw us and the likelihood of seeing a bear was greatly diminished with Butch by your side. On day seven, I would learn Butch's heart is as big as his voice. He did not have an alarm to wake him up, so most mornings you could hear someone yelling, "Butch, it's time to get up." Day seven has already been talked about, but I want to talk about it from what I witnessed from Butch that day. As mentioned before, my brother Jon was struggling, but his struggle pales in comparison to how bad Shawn was hurting. Shawn had been struggling since day one and would come to camp each night too exhausted to eat. Butch was running a little late that morning. While we all took off for the long day ahead, he and Shawn were in the back together and we would not see them again until they made it into camp around 9:00 that night. The last several miles they hiked with one headlamp between the two of them. Shawn was ready to quit several times that day, but Butch stayed by his side and encouraged him the whole way. Unless you have experienced something like this, you really can't understand how exhausting it is to not only hike yourself, but to do everything you can to keep someone else motivated. It is impossible to get into any kind of rhythm when you are hiking in this manner. Later in the hike, Butch would give me the same kind of encouragement when I begin to experience the muscle fatigue towards the end of each day. Ironically, the last couple of days of our journey, it was Butch who would need inspiration from others in the group because of the punishing knee pain he was undergoing.

Butch took full advantage of every opportunity he had to share with fellow hikers why we were hiking. We were on a mission to raise money for missions. I remember coming down Mt. Whitney with him, as we stopped to talk to a father and his two sons right at the Whitney portal. They were enjoying a lunch and soaking in the fact they had just finished the JMT. Most people travel south on the hike, which allows them to complete the expedition with a monumental trek up Whitney. We stopped for a good fifteen minutes while Butch shared everything he knew about MANNA. It was also on this day, I realized Butch and I shared another passion, which was to win. When we finally hit the path again, the father and his sons said, "Well, I'm sure we will catch you soon." My competitive spirit was shaken to the core in that moment, but I didn't say anything because I didn't know Butch very well yet. About four miles later we were close to the bottom of the hill, when we heard the trio behind us. At that moment, I knew Butch and I would be life-long friends. Suddenly, our pace picked up as we flew down the trail. Later, I asked him, "Did you pick up the pace so those guys wouldn't catch us?" He responded with "Oh yeah."

His heart for suffering people was highly evident on day seven. This was the whole reason we were on this excursion. He was the only one on the hike who was not a pastor or missionary, but his passion for rescuing children from the grip of poverty was evident. Where does this kind of love and passion originate? From where does this kind of empathy come? His booming voice telling others about our mission and his resounding love, is evidence of a man who has been touched by the heart of Jesus. When you are hurting physically, emotionally and spiritually; it is something special knowing you will not be abandoned.

Mount Calvary

Golgotha, Calvary or The Skull are a few of the names we have come to know as Mt. Calvary. The climb up Mt. Calvary would provide life for all who believe. The climb up Mt. Calvary would divide history. The climb up Mt. Calvary was the toughest climb anyone has ever made. The climb up Mt. Calvary is where the Son would be abandoned by the Father. The climb up Mt. Calvary changed everything! In his book, *The Mountains Are Calling*, Jarrett Stephens points out three ways that Jesus suffered.

1. Jesus Suffered Physically

The Romans did not invent the crucifixion, but it has been said by many they perfected this form of torture which inevitably led to death. Before Jesus would be nailed to the cross, He would have to survive the unimaginable pain of being flogged.

> The usual instrument was a short whip with several single or braided leather thongs of variable lengths, in which small iron balls or sharp pieces of sheep bones were tied at intervals. For scourging, the man was stripped of his clothing, and his hands were tied to an upright post. The back, buttocks, and legs were flogged

either by two soldiers (lictors) or by one who alternated positions. The severity of the scourging depended on the disposition of the lictors and was intended to weaken the victim to a state just short of collapse or death. As the Roman soldiers repeatedly struck the victim's back with full force, the iron balls would cause deep contusions, and the leather thongs and sheep bones would cut into the skin and subcutaneous tissues. Then, as the flogging continued, the lacerations would tear into the underlying skeletal muscles and produce quivering ribbons of bleeding flesh. Pain and blood loss generally set the stage for circulatory shock. The extent of blood loss may well have determined how long the victim would survive on the cross. After the scourging, the soldiers often taunted their victim."[1]

This experience would eventually filet the back of the one being flogged. We read in the Bible; Jesus was not even recognizable as a man. Jesus would then be expected to carry the cross beam of the cross, which would weigh somewhere between 75 to 125 pounds. Jesus was so weak at this point, they summoned Simon to carry the cross up the hill to the top of the mountain. Once they reached the

[1] "The Physical Death of Jesus Christ," JAMA, March 21, 1986, Vol. 255, No. 11.

final place of the crucifixion, they would nail our Savior to the cross. Crucifixion was one of the most disgraceful and cruel methods of execution: which was usually reserved only for slaves, foreigners, revolutionaries, and the vilest of criminals.

2. Jesus Suffered Emotionally

I'm sure you have experienced betrayal on some level in your life, but Jesus would be betrayed by one of His disciples for thirty pieces of silver. Mark tells us once Jesus was arrested, the rest of the disciples scattered. We all know the story of Peter's denial. Peter denied him, not once, not twice, but three times. The men he had poured His life into over the last three years, left Him to face his accusers alone. *"Consider the emotional impact of having his creation call for his execution."*[2]

3. Jesus Suffered Spiritually

This is where the ultimate suffering came into play. Not only did Jesus suffer physically and emotionally, but he also suffered spiritually. Let's read how Mark describes some of His last words.

---

[2] Jarrett Stephens, *The Mountains are Calling: Making the Climb for a Clearer View of God and Ourselves* (Colorado Springs: Multnomah, 2018), 139.

And when the sixth hour had come, there was darkness over the whole land until the ninth hour. And at the ninth hour Jesus cried with a loud voice, "Eloi, Eloi, lema sabachthani?" which means, "My God, my God, why have you forsaken me? (Mark 15:33–34)

This cry has been referred to as the "cry of desertion." The Trinity is something every human will fall short in trying to describe, but one thing we see repeatedly in Scripture is the unity existing in the Trinity. While on the cross, Jesus took on the iniquity of us all. He took all my sin and the guilt attached to it. He took all your sin and the shame you bare. The weight of the sins of the world had to be unbearable. Therefore, Jesus died of a broken heart. Not only was he carrying the burden of our sin, but the affliction of being abandoned by His Father. "Jesus was not just feeling abandoned by God at Calvary; he was abandoned by God"[3] In this moment, He who knew no sin, became sin so you can I could be made righteous. While suffering physical, emotional and spiritual agony; Jesus was left abandoned and alone.

Did you know while the soldiers and the Savior walked up the hill to Calvary there was a messenger, walking in front of them, holding a sign? History tells us the messenger

[3] Stephens, *The Mountains are Calling*, 141.

would carry the sign, which proclaimed the crime of the accused. This sign was known as the accusation. Once they reached the top of the mountain, they would nail the sign to the cross above the head of the one being executed. The sign was a proclamation of the crime and guilt of the criminal. John says,

> **John 19:18–22**, There they crucified him, and with him two others, one on either side, and Jesus between them. Pilate also wrote an inscription and put it on the cross. It read, "Jesus of Nazareth, the King of the Jews." Many of the Jews read this inscription, for the place where Jesus was crucified was near the city, and it was written in Aramaic, in Latin, and in Greek. So the chief priests of the Jews said to Pilate, "Do not write, 'The King of the Jews,' but rather, 'This man said, I am King of the Jews.'" Pilate answered, "What I have written I have written."

I think Pilate knew exactly what he was doing. He had found no guilt in Jesus, so he purposefully proclaimed Him as the King of the Jews. The gospel message was displayed loudly above the Messiah who made the Good News possible on that fateful day. This sign showed no sin. His accusation screamed His innocence to the crowd who screamed for His execution. His accusation declared the lengths God would go to redeem His children. His accusation broadcasted His love for you.

You know what else was nailed to the cross that day? My sin! Your Sin! The sins of the whole world were nailed to the cross along with our Savior. Read the letter Paul sent to the Colossian church.

> **Colossians 2:13–15,** And you, who were dead in your trespasses and the uncircumcision of your flesh, God made alive together with him, having forgiven us all our trespasses, by canceling the record of debt that stood against us with its legal demands. This he set aside, nailing it to the cross. He disarmed the rulers and authorities and put them to open shame, by triumphing over them in him."

Jesus went to the cross to pay for your sins. Three days later, they would find an empty tomb which shows us that the payment He made was sufficient for the sins committed. The legal demands for our sins have all been met. You have not committed one sin, nor will commit, in which Jesus did not pay. Why would Jesus do this for us? Why would He go through that much suffering? Why would the innocent be slain for the guilty? Jesus walked up the mountain of agony, so you and I could be set free. Jesus climbed the mountain of shame and suffering so we would no longer suffer from our shame. If you have never trusted in His payment for your sins, I pray you will be overcome with the knowledge His grace is free. You simply need to put your faith in Him. As Christians, we need to stop walking in or guilt and shame. It can be tiring to think that we need to continue to earn God's forgiveness or approval. Every day, we need to learn to trust the completed work of Christ on the cross. You are forgiven, accepted, loved and have been set free by the work of Jesus. Walk in freedom! When we choose to walk in the freedom of Christ, it allows us to move past our guilt and shame. When we choose to walk in freedom, we are aware we do not walk alone, and have not been abandoned. Walking in this freedom gives us the courage, when God calls us to the mountain to say, *I MUST GO!*

CHAPTER 10—Mountaintop Mandate

Michael's Tale from the Trail

Day eight was scheduled to be one of our easiest days of the hike. We thought the day might be easy and it actually was. We spent most of the morning hiking down a moderate decline, which would take us down the well-known Golden Staircase. Andrew, Joey, Butch and I stopped at a beautiful rock overhang, which provided a nice cool shade to eat our lunch. The rest of the group had stopped about a mile back to eat, and the plan was to meet up with them at our campsite approximately three miles up the trail. Shawn was still struggling from the long day he had the day before. Lonnie offered to take his tent and some of his gear for him so the last part of the hike would be a little easier. Shawn promised he would make it to the campsite if they left him behind to rest a little longer.

It was only 2:00 in the afternoon and we had already arrived at our resting spot for the night. To this point of our trip, this was the earliest we would set up, and we would never make it that early again. Lonnie and I set up Shawn's tent with the hope that he would show up soon. Around 3:00 that afternoon it began to rain, which turned into a light hailstorm. It is unreal to think back on how God allowed us to hike in such beautiful weather. Safe inside our tents, most of us took a long nap while our tents were being peppered with rain and hail. Once the storm passed over, we all emerged from our sleep to make dinner. Our spot for the night was close to Evolution Creek, which was raging. I remember scooting down a slippery rock next to a rushing waterfall to try and get water for the night. Jon and I looked at each other thinking, out of all the things we would do on this hike, the most dangerous was getting water here at this very spot.

As time went by, we began to get a little more concerned with whether Shawn was going to make it that night. Several times, Lonnie walked a mile or two back down the trail yelling his name. We asked every hiker that passed by our tents if they had seen him. Not a word. We all went to bed praying at some point we would hear Shawn stumble into camp, and we could point him to his tent. I don't know how many times Lonnie went looking for him, but I'm sure he didn't sleep well all night. Once the day broke, we gathered to pray and discuss what we would do. Lonnie and Andrew made the decision to head back down the path to look for Shawn. Ironically, they found him bundled up in his sleeping bag under the same rock that four of us had eaten lunch the day before. Once Shawn saw Lonnie, he was overcome with emotion. He had pushed himself past his limits in every imaginable way. They made plans for him to get to the ranger station so he could take some time to regain his strength and figure out a plan to hike out. We would learn a day later; he was so sick that he had to be medevacked out by helicopter. The reason I tell you this story is because Shawn was alone and hopeless, but the moment he saw Lonnie and Andrew he knew he would be okay. His exact words to Lonnie were, "I knew you would come back for me." Lonnie was on a mission to rescue his friend. The whole purpose for this hike was a mission to rescue kids from the grip of poverty. Physical food is only half of MANNA's rescue mission. We want these kids across the globe to understand they are not alone. Jesus came for them. Jesus came for you. Jesus came for me. Jesus came to rescue all of us from our sins. As Christians, we are all on a rescue mission.

Jon's Tale from the Trail

I have a habit of walking in the back. I have taken many trips overseas and into large cities with groups on mission trips. I walk in the back so I can keep my eyes on people and make sure everyone arrives safe and sound. I found myself naturally doing the same exact thing on the hike. Bringing up the rear in a large group on a long trail, brings a lot of interesting conversations. Andrew, our fearless leader, who earned the trail-name "Mountain Goat" was in the lead many days. Andrew is a Vice President of MANNA Worldwide. MANNA is the organization behind our hike. The official name of our hike was #FeedThe-Need, MANNA's Hike for Hunger. Andrew has passion for feeding kids both physically and spiritually. He carried with him laminated cards that hung from the back of his pack. He had taken pictures of kids from the Guatemala orphanage in which we were raising money. The hike proved to be a great opportunity to talk with people about MANNA and the need to rescue kids from the grips of poverty. Keith, a training partner and one of the people who hiked the first five days with us, had his daughter make me a sign. I walked many days to the church office from my home as I was training, and I hung her sign on the back of my pack. The sign had the logo for the hike, as well as the website for MANNA. I decided to leave the sign on my pack for the duration of the hike. Many days when people would pass me, they would have already had four or five conversations about the mission we were completing. They were impressed and humbled we would take this challenge on for the mission of rescuing kids from the grip of poverty. My sign was a constant reminder of why I was doing what I was doing. Conversely, the sign was often a frustration. The wind would catch it and blow it all over the place. Every time I needed to get something out of my pack, it was in the way. However, every time I needed to get something out of my pack, it was a reminder of the reason I was hiking. The mission is to not only rescue kids from the grip of poverty, but from the grip of sin. The mission is to let them know Jesus loves them and He offers forgiveness through His amazing grace. He gave the mission to the disciples on top of, you guessed it, a mountain. The mountain is never named in scripture. While the name of the mountain is insignificant, it was the mandate on the mountain that would change the world.

Mount No Name

Eric Lindell, known most from the movie about his life, *Chariots of Fire,* was a dedicated man of faith. He would win gold in the 1924 Olympics in Paris. He gave his life to fulfill the mandate. He was driven by this mandate. He was passionate about living his life on a mission to fulfill God's mission. You can sense the passion in his writing.

> Jesus' life is the most beautiful life there has ever been ... They (the disciples) failed him at his death, but with the resurrection and Pentecost they awoke to the meaning of the message he had been trying to give them, and went out to conquer the world.[1]

Let's look at this mandate given on top of the unnamed mountain.

> **Matthew 28:16–20**, Now the eleven disciples went to Galilee, to the mountain to which Jesus had directed them. And when they saw him, they worshiped him, but some doubted. And Jesus came and said to them, "All authority in heaven and on earth has been given to me. Go therefore

[1] Daniel L. Akin, *10 Who Changed the World* (Nashville: B&H, 2012),124.

and make disciples of all nations, baptizing them in the name of the Father and of the Son and of the Holy Spirit, teaching them to observe all that I have commanded you. And behold, I am with you always, to the end of the age."

Jesus came to proclaim the Kingdom of God, to offer His blessing to those who would take heed, and to instruct people in its obligations and responsibilities. When he left, he committed the duty of carrying on the work to the church. The church is His voice in the world, announcing the Good News about God. The church calls men everywhere to repent and invites them to enter the Kingdom of God. Every follower of Jesus shares this responsibility.

The mission of the church is to make disciples. The vision of the church I serve is to lead people to find and follow Jesus. Let me take a minute to give you a simple definition of these words. Dr. Tony Evans definition of a disciple is, *"a visible verbal follower of Jesus."* I love this simple definition which implies if we are a true follower of Jesus, we live like Jesus and tell people about Him. We talk most about what we love most. The vision of leading people to find and follow Jesus involves two aspects: evangelism and discipleship. Let me give you a brief definition of those two words. Evangelism is sharing the gospel by public preaching and personal witness.

Discipleship is intentionally equipping believers to be faithful followers of Jesus.

Back to the nameless mountain. Jesus had laid his life down and died a horrible death on Mt. Calvary. He had been placed in a borrowed tomb and victoriously arose on the third day. He is on top of the mountain and would soon ascend into heaven. His last mandate to his disciple is simple: *GO MAKE DISCIPLES* of all nations. We are to lead people to find and follow Jesus globally and locally. This mission is meant to be lived out in community and in partnership. I cannot make disciples of all nations by myself.

Let's not get hung up on the word, "GO!" I think most of us read the word and infer that GOING is for someone else. The reality of this mandate is we are all supposed to make disciples. All believers are to make disciples! For that to happen, we will have to decide if we will get involved in the process of evangelism and discipleship. Eric Liddell said it this way, *"I need a Savior to save me from the guilt of sin; to save me from the power of sin. I need a Savior whose grace is sufficient to enable me to live a life of unselfish service and love."*[2]

Jesus is not giving them or us a simple task. This is a monumental task. This is the task of a lifetime. *"Based on the verb tense and wording of the Greek text, Jesus was*

[2] Akin, *10 Who Changed the World*, 132.

saying: As you go, MAKE DISCIPLES. "[3] The emphasis is on making disciples, not going. What if you looked at this verse as it was intended? The perspective would change. Generally, followers of Jesus read this verse with the emphasis on the word "GO!" Therefore, they transfer the mandate to be to those who are called to go somewhere else. The mission is to make disciples as you go, wherever you go, or on your way to where you are going. We are all supposed to make disciples as we go, but this means helping those who are called to go to the "uttermost" parts of the world.

This brings me back to the hike. We endured many long days. I experienced many long nights in my tent asking God for strength and power. God also provided moments to remind us why we were on this hike in the first place. The mandate was to make disciples of all nations. If we are going to fulfill the mandate, we need to partner with others. Bruce, O'Neal is the founder and CEO of MANNA Worldwide, and happens to be a member of the church I pastor. He was saved at our church in the late 1970's and Raymond Dunn, my grandfather in-law, baptized him. God placed a calling for him to GO and make disciples internationally. He faithfully ministered in Metro Manila, Philippines for nearly 17 years. He started a feeding center

[3] Jarrett Stephens, *The Mountains are Calling: Making the Climb for a Clearer View of God and Ourselves* (Colorado Springs: Multnomah, 2018), 156.

out of his church and God blessed it. He felt God leading him to start another one on the other side of Manila and God blessed it as well. Bruce and his remarkable wife, Pam, made the toughest decision of their life, to move back to Texas. God was calling them to something much bigger. The decision to start MANNA WORLDWIDE was made 19 years ago. They now feed 14,000 kids each day in 50 different countries. WOW! God blessed their step of faith. Therefore, we were hiking. These kids need food, water, and a place to go to church. These kids need Jesus. The hike was a way to provide money for people to go tell the kids, whose pictures were hanging from Andrew's pack, that God loves them. This reminds me of what Paul wrote in Romans chapter ten.

Romans 10:13, For everyone who calls on the name of the Lord will be saved.

The statement is not a question, but a declaration. The declarative statement is that WHOEVER calls on the name of the Lord, shall be saved. The statement does not say, they might be saved, but SHALL or WILL be saved. This is great news! Paul, through the inspiration of God, says anyone who calls on the name of Jesus will be saved. However, let's take a moment to read the next few verses.

Romans 10:14–15, How then will they call on him in whom they have not believed? And how are they to believe in him of whom they have never heard? And how are they to hear without someone preaching? And how are they to preach unless they are sent? As it is written, "How beautiful are the feet of those who preach the good news!"

Paul ask four questions in these two verses. They are thought-provoking, rhetorical questions. The answer is obvious. He is not looking for you to answer the question, but to see the greater truth revealed through the questions. The four questions are:

1. How can they call on Him in whom they have not believed?
2. How can they believe in Him of whom they have not heard?
3. How can they hear without a preacher? (someone who speaks)
4. How can they preach unless they are sent?

Jesus had mandated we are to make disciples. This mandate is to all believers and as we go, we are to be involved in the process of leading people to find and follow Jesus. God may not want me to go to Kenya, but he does want me to make disciples of all nations. Therefore, if he has not called me to go to Kenya, I should help those who have been called to go to Kenya. As I make disciples, I can also help others make disciples.

John and Betty Stam were missionaries to communist China in the 1930's. They lived a short-dedicated life to Jesus. They were both beheaded, at the ages of 28 and 27, and their bodies were left for days in the streets of China. The night before, Betty tucked her three-month-old baby into a dresser in the back of a closet at the house they were being detained. Praise the Lord, the baby was found and brought back to live with family. John once wrote, *"The faithfulness of God is the only certain thing in the world today. We need not fear the result of trusting Him."*[4] The world needs more people like John and Betty who are willing to make disciples as they go and wherever they go. Let me share with you a poem written by Betty:

Open my eyes, that I may see
This one and that one needing Thee,
Hearts that are dumb, unsatisfied,
Lives that are dead, for who Christ died.

Open my eyes in sympathy,
clear into man's deep soul to see;

[4] Akin, *10 Who Changed the World*, 139.

Wise with thy wisdom to discern,
and with the heart of love to yearn.

Open my eyes in faith, I pray;
Give me strength to speak today,
Someone to bring, dear Lord, to Thee:
Use me, O Lord, use even me.[5]

As you go MAKE DISCIPLES of all nations; this was the clear and concise mandate in which Jesus gave his disciples then and today.

On this unnamed mountain, we find that the Christian life is not meant to be a solo climb in order to meet with God and remain in some kind of holy huddle atop that mountain. Instead, it's on the mountain that our hearts and visions are enlarged to see how great the love of God is, and how much a lost and hurting world needs to experience it. We are forever changed, and as we go back down the mountain, we are compelled to share with others this message of hope that has affected us in such incredible ways. We leave the mountain on a mission with a mandate from Jesus.[6]

[5] Akin, *10 Who Changed the World*, 145.
[6] Stephens, *The Mountains are Calling*, 164.

The disciples left the mountain that day on a mission with a mandate. They were to go to Jerusalem and wait to be empowered by the Spirit of God. The book of Acts speaks of the moment they received the power of God. The Spirit of God empowered them to go make disciples. Believers today are empowered by the same spirit and need to be fueled by the same passion to fulfill the mandate given on the unnamed mountain. Is it possible today you could do more to help make disciples all over the world? I remember bending down in the cool, wet grass on day five at Rae Lakes. The scene was surreal and unbelievably breathtaking. I knelt to fill my water bottle up to have water for breakfast in the morning. I was using a Sawyer water filter. I immediately had a flashback. I was suddenly transported to northern Romania walking the dirt streets of a Gypsy village. The people were poor and lacked necessities. However, the kids were anxious to play and to meet the people from America. I was holding a large five-gallon bucket with a Sawyer water filter attached to it. The team gathered in the house of an older lady who was surrounded by kids covered in dirt. The team gave a quick demonstration on how to use this water filter system. Their lives would be changed because of this one gift. They would not only receive clean water, but they would receive living water, Jesus. Back to Rae Lakes. The sun would be setting soon, and my water bottles were full for the next morning.

I climbed into my tent and tucked myself into my sleeping bag, thinking about what I just experienced. The water I was filtering was crystal clear snow run-off. The kids who needed these filters, had been drinking from the sewer run-off. I found new motivation. This hike was more than a hike. This was an opportunity to #FeedTheNeed. This was an opportunity to raise funds and awareness for kids who need water and thirst for Jesus. The mandate was given, and the mountains are calling, *I MUST GO!*

CONCLUSION

Mountaintop moments inspire us to know Him more, but the second part of the adventure comes when we descend the mountain and share the information and inspiration with others. My brother and I have revealed our struggles, our joys, our pain, and our triumphs. I desire as you read this book, God revealed Himself to you in a real and personal way, and you will descend the mountain so you can relay what God has taught you. I pray this book took you on an epic journey of knowing God and finding purpose.

God is real and He knows my name. This may be the greatest takeaway for me. This is a truth I have been taught my entire life but, on this hike, I experienced it in a new way. Day four started with a lot of doubt in my mind. We had summitted Whitney the day before and as we were getting to Guitar Lake, which was two miles into the Whitney ascent, I started having a stabbing pain in my left knee.

This was supposed to be my good knee. Luckily, Nick, our friend from the UK, had a knee brace he let me wear the entire day. I was not sure if I would be able to make the next 14 days. Day five would be my last good opportunity to exit the trail and ride back with my friend, Keith. I decided if I could get over Forrester Pass on day four, God would allow me to make it. Praise the Lord! I had no knee pain on day four. The hike down the backside of Forrester Pass was very long and seemed to have an endless number of switchbacks. Before I tell you how the rest of the hike went, let me take a side trail.

> **John 20:11–16,** But Mary stood outside by the tomb weeping, and as she wept, she stooped down *and looked* into the tomb. And she saw two angels in white sitting, one at the head and the other at the feet, where the body of Jesus had lain. Then they said to her, "Woman, why are you weeping?" She said to them, "Because they have taken away my Lord, and I do not know where they have laid Him." Now when she had said this, she turned around and saw Jesus standing *there,* and did not know that it was Jesus. Jesus said to her, "Woman, why are you weeping? Whom are you seeking?" She, supposing Him to be the gardener, said to Him, "Sir, if You have carried Him

away, tell me where You have laid Him, and I will take Him away." Jesus said to her, **"Mary!"** She turned and said to Him, "Rabboni!" (which is to say, Teacher).

Have you ever thought about the fact that Jesus knows your name? The Bible says He created you in your mother's womb and knew you even before you were conceived. The Bible tells us the Lord collects your tears in a bottle and He knows the hairs on your head. The details the Lord knows about you are unreal. Jesus spoke the name of Mary and this changed everything for her. She immediately knew He was alive, and He was the Messiah. He was who He had said He was, and He knew her name.

The Lord knew Abram's name and changed it to Abraham. He changed Jacob's name to Israel, Saul to Paul and Sarai to Sarah. The Lord knows your name. He loves you so much, He chose to climb Calvary's mountain in order to make a way for you to get to God. I am convinced God interacts with us much more than we are aware. A few years ago, a lady in my church named Sarah McLemore, handed me a poem on Easter Sunday. She told me she had been praying over the poem for a year but had been unable to finish the last stanza. She wanted to write an Easter poem, but it had sat unfinished for the whole year. God had finally given her the last stanza and she was convinced it was from Him.

Let's go back to the mountain. I felt a little dizzy and lightheaded coming down Forrester Pass. Michael and I came over the pass together. We stopped so I could eat some trail mix and drink some water, hoping it would take away my dizziness. As we began the journey down, Michael was ready to pick up the pace. I told him I was fine, and he could speed up if he wanted. Shawn and Craig were behind me still so I felt it would be a good time for us both to have some time to hike alone.

Another hour passed and the switchbacks just kept coming. The shadows were in and out that day, as they passed back and forth out of the sun, making my way down the dry, rocky pass. The dizziness subsided for a little while, but then it came back with a vengeance. I'm not sure if I was dealing with altitude sickness, motion sickness, low blood sugar or possibly drinking bacteria from improperly filtered water. No matter the cause for my sickness, it had become quite a concern. The back and forth had me very lightheaded and dizzy. Let me share Sarah's Easter poem.

THE CROWN AND THE CROSS

A crown of thorns upon His head
Beads of blood peppering down,
He went to the cross in my stead
And for me He wore that crown

Nails were hammered through each hand
And a spear was plunged into His side,
Limply He hung, unable to stand.
Freely, He bled, freely, He died.

Father, forgive them for they know not what
they do.
Then this His final plea
I commend my Spirit to You
And with that, His Spirit was free.

The earth shook and the thunder rolled
As His lifeless body hung there
Then the curtain was rent in two
In the synagogue of prayer

They took His body from the cross
And laid it in a borrowed tomb
Guarded by soldiers against loss,
It lay three days in this womb

On the morning of the third day
The woman hurried to the grave
They found the stone rolled away
And just the burial cloth there lay

Why do you look for the living among the dead?
Asked the angel at the grave
He has risen as He said
Come and see the place where he lay

They looked and saw, and they cried
For his body was not there
Just the grave cloths lay inside-
Otherwise the tomb was bare

Mary was distraught, bereft
Thinking Jesus had been removed
Heartbroken, the women wept
As they stood just outside the tomb.

Please, Sir, if you've removed Him,
Just tell us where and I'll go there.
**Then Jesus called her by name
And the world was never the same.**

—Sarah McLemore

Sarah handed me her poem. I quickly put it in my Bible as I rushed to get ready for our Easter service beginning to start. Remember, she had taken a year to finish this poem and it was all hinging on the last two lines. The message I preached was on the resurrection, which is a typical Easter sermon. I ended the sermon that morning by reading the above passage of scripture. The climactic finish to my sermon was the following statement. **Jesus called her by name, and the world was never the same.** She came up to me after the service and said, "Did you read the poem?" I said, "Not yet." "You must read it. You have to read it", she said with such enthusiasm. God speaks to us all the time and we often don't listen or respond. This amazing lady waited for a year to finish her poem. On Easter Sunday, God revealed to her He was speaking directly to her. He knew her and He knew her name.

Let me finish the story from the hike. "*JON!*" Someone yelled my name and snapped me out of my trance. I woke up, realizing I was about to miss the turn on the switchback and walk off the side of the mountain. You know what? No one was within a mile of me on that mountain side. I was completely by myself, but not alone. God was with me. He was not only with me; He knew my name and that changed everything. I am convinced, now more than ever when He calls my name to take another step of faith and to climb another mountain, I will confidently say, *I MUST GO!*

MOUNTAIN MOMENTS

Shawn Lutgen

Proverbs 16:9, "The mind of man plans his way, But the LORD directs his steps."

Things don't always happen the way you plan. Prior to turning 50, my friend and co-worker Lonnie Lehrman said, "We need to do something special for our birthdays." Weeks later the plan was revealed. "We're going to hike the John Muir Trail for a MANNA WORLDWIDE fundraiser," he said. I was in immediately. Like the rest of the guys going: training ensued, YouTube was binged, and gear was gathered. I knew the hike would be challenging, so I worked hard to get ready. The days checked off the calendar and I was soon taking my first steps on the trail.

I'll admit, I am not fast. We had ambitious mileage goals each day, and too often I was running out of day before I ran out of miles. Hiking from dark to dark on several days, exhausting myself physically, mentally and topping it off with poor nutrition was a bad combination. Each evening I arrived at camp exhausted, knowing I needed to eat, but equally just wanting to crash. I would choke down a few bites of something, situate my sleep system and I would be out.

On day nine, it was like a switch flipped. It was a level of exhaustion I had never felt before. I was alone, discouraged, hurting, and the thought of ending my hike was so disappointing, but I knew something wasn't right.

Just before my episode, I caught up with the group. They had their break, and I was beginning mine. Guys started heading off. Lonnie asked if he could carry my tent. I gave it to him. He asked if I was okay. I was tired, but okay. We only had about six more miles left that day. I was sure I could make it. Jon Haley was the last one to leave. I told him to go on ahead. It was soon after, the switch flipped.

I'll spare the details of my body eliminating its contents. I was grateful to have trees to hide behind. I moved on and stopped to get water, sat down against a tree and woke up about an hour later. I pressed on knowing I only had about four miles to go. My body continued to send me signals saying, "You have to stop." A few minutes later a hiker came by and asked if I was ok. "I don't think so." I said. He asked if I was with anyone. I told him, "Yes, but they're an hour or more ahead of me." He got my name and took off running.

My breathing changed, I was lightheaded, my back and legs were cramped up, and I was dry heaving. I was afraid to move, because I knew if I did, I would hit the ground. Later a man and his daughter came through. "Are you Shawn?", he asked. I told him yes and he said they had met a guy going the opposite direction looking for the guys in my group. He suggested I lay down. I got down on the ground, propped my feet up and everything seemed to close in around me. I laid there staring up through the trees into a cloudy sky. I heard some thunder in the distance as little sprinkles of rain began to fall. I was thinking about my wife, Chrissy, and my boys, while wondering, "How will I get out of here?"

Other people stopped by, including a paramedic from Dallas, TX. She checked my vitals, gave me an aspirin, some honey, and made a high sodium broth. I started feeling better. But like other evenings out on the trail, I was once again running out of daylight. The thought then came to me, "Lonnie has my tent." I shared that information with the group around and one of them mentioned there was a big rock just up the trail which had a perfect shelter area underneath it. I got to my feet after sitting up for a while and a guy from Paris, France carried my pack and followed behind me as I walked to my home for the night. As I was getting settled in a couple came walking by, they commented on how incredible my accommodations were.

The lady said, "I feel like the Lord is telling me to sing you a song." She sang, "Jesus, Jesus, Jesus, sweetest name I know, fills my every longing, and keeps me singing as I go." They continued down the trail, and I put my face in my hands, shed some tears of gratefulness, and prayed.

When you're out in an area like that, it's amazing how heightened your senses become. I was all bedded down in something which resembles a place where a big, furry friend may live, hoping he didn't come home for the night. Lying there with a pile of rocks and my open knife beside me, I looked at my map and made a plan to hike to the ranger station the next morning, take a zero day, and then hike out over Bishop Pass. Here, I could rent a car and drive home. It was a solid plan, so I thought.

I headed out the next morning. I was confident I would run into the group or at least some of them again. As I came over a hill I heard, "Shawn!" It was Lonnie and Andrew. I told Lonnie, "I knew you would come back." I briefly explained what all had happened and that I needed to get off the trail. Lonnie offered to leave with me, and I told him, "No, I want you to finish." I shared my plan and we prayed together. They went on to complete the last days of the hike, and I went on to find my way home. I made it to the ranger station. I shared my story, she checked my vitals, consulted doctors in town, and it was decided that hiking out alone was not a good idea. She said there was a train of horses that pass through every now and then, or I could get a helicopter. I asked, "How much is that helicopter?" She said in California it was free. "Let's get a helicopter then", I said. Later that afternoon, a California Highway Patrol helicopter, including a new friend named Rusty, made an amazing landing among the trees and gave me a scenic flight to a hospital in Fresno, CA. In the ER, they started with lots of questions and blood work. There were protein enzymes in my blood. They were concerned about them, as they could be signs of a heart attack. After x-rays, echocardiogram, and a nuclear stress test, the results came back negative. "You're the healthiest sick person I've ever met", one doctor said. My diagnosis was Rhabdomyolisis, a breakdown of muscle tissue that releases a damaging protein into the blood which leads to kidney failure. I was fortunate to have left the trail when I did.

A local church from our fellowship of churches contacted me, so I had an exit strategy ready whenever they discharged me. What I didn't know was one more event needed to happen. When I was taken to my hospital room on day two, it was the kind you share with another person, divided by a curtain. My roommate's name was Gabriel and he was in bad shape. He couldn't get out of bed and slept most of the time. He was completely alone. He had no family or friends. He lived by himself and didn't drive. This guy was alone and probably close to death. I was about to be discharged on day three. I went over to Gabriel's side of the room to go into the restroom. Like usual he was asleep. I prayed asking God to give me a chance to talk to him before I left. When I came out, he was awake and greeted me with a hello. I said, "Gabriel, you have the same name as an important angel in the Bible." He began to cry. I asked him, "Gabriel, do you know Jesus?" With a smile through his tears he said, "Oh, I know Jesus." We had a great conversation and prayer. I then went and sat on my bed and prayed, "If I had to go through everything for this moment, to encourage a person, completely alone, possibly soon before he passes away, I'd do it again."

As I look back on my JMT, Hike for Hunger, I've come to some conclusions.

Preparation is vital. Teamwork is essential. You are stronger than you realize. The Rock will provide. Your destination may be different than what you had planned. I had prepared, trained, traveled, hiked, and hurt to feed kids around the world. Was it all so that I could meet a guy named Gabriel, or maybe he was sent there for me? Things don't always happen the way you plan.

Craig Alsup

As a full-time missionary Assistant Director for Asia with MANNA Worldwide, I was more than beyond thrilled when I heard there would be a thru-hike of the John Muir Trail. As soon as the hike was announced, I signed up and began to think about and prepare for the hike. I knew that it would be difficult, as I had taken on long and tough hikes before. In 2005, I hiked 550 miles of the Appalachian Trail from Georgia to Virginia. Some moments of that trail were a suffer fest, but many of the memories were so great, I fully expected the JMT to be much the same. I mean, what could be better? Almost three weeks of hiking in beautiful mountain scenery, sleeping under the stars, getting to spend time with church and business leaders from around the country, and getting to do it all as part of my mission to rescue kids from the grip of poverty . . . Sign me up!

Over the next several months, I began to dust off my old hiking gear, narrow it down to reduce pack weight, purchase items in the United States as well as during mission trips in Nepal, break in my new trail runners, and douse everything in bug repellant. I did crazy things: like cut tags and extra straps off of gear to lighten it, mix food bags full of dehydrated ingredients, and go on long, hot hikes in the heat of the Texas summer to prepare my body.

Years earlier, when hiking in Nepal to reach Mount Everest base camp, my wife and I had done much of the same preparation to stand at the foot of the world's tallest mountain. We began the hike at close to 10,000 feet above sea level, a place where we had never been up until that time. The hike was grueling but afforded incredible views throughout. We were loving every second of it. At least, we were until we began to feel sluggish, queasy, and more and more out of breath. We began to struggle with basic tasks such as dressing, eating and drinking, carrying our backpacks, and even things as simple as tying our shoes. After several days hiking towards Mount Everest, we had to abandon our hope to reach basecamp as we were told by local guides that we must turn back or face extreme sickness and possibly death. We headed down the mountain, broken and looking for a reason and some recovery.

We found it in a town called Pokhara in an area of Nepal we never planned to visit. What happened over the next month was nothing short of God showing us our plans are often not His plans, but His plans are always for our good. We found an orphanage and began to volunteer, which led to us falling in love with and beginning to sponsor two children, Aasha and Sagar, who have since become members of our family. We met a man named Binod who became our very first missionary partner and with whom we have developed a bond as family. I truly believe that God got me off that mountain to lead me into a valley to help me to realize His plan for me to become a missionary.

That hike has become a part of our story, just like I'm sure this one will. As we headed toward our first campsite for this hike, I was giddy with excitement about the experience to come. I prayed leading up to this trip God would protect me from the same altitude sickness that took me off the trail to Everest. I took medications to prepare my body for the altitude. It wasn't enough. Day one left me tired and already beginning to recognize the effects of the altitude on my body. Day two afforded beautiful views I struggled to even notice because my body was revolting against the daily grind at altitudes over 10,000 feet. As the days progressed, I realized that the thru-hike of the JMT may not happen for me. I was heartbroken and confused. I tried to push my body daily to complete the miles, but struggled to eat and drink enough, so I began to dehydrate quickly walking many miles and many hours each day.

I looked around me at those in our party who seemed to be taking it all in stride, and at times, I admit I was jealous. What did they do that I didn't do? What gift did they have that I didn't have? If God got me off Everest so that He could show me the purpose of my life from that point on, then why was He getting me off this mountain?

On my final night on the trail, I lay awake all-night writhing in agony and praying for God to make it subside.

As those around me slept, I wept and asked God for help and healing. On my final day on the trail, I awoke early and headed out. The miles passed quickly, but my body was already drained because of dehydration and lack of sleep the night before. I made it to a big climb up a switch-back covered mountain and began to climb, knowing it would take hours.

During the climb, I was forced to stop every 3–5 steps to catch my breath while leaning on my trekking poles. I prayed a lot. I cried a little. I thought of the faces of the children that we serve with MANNA Worldwide and tried to use that as fuel to press on. By the top of the climb, I made the decision to stop, pray, and wait on someone else to catch up to me to help me flesh out a decision of what I should do. The top of this climb represented a decision point, a final option to get off trail before moving further away from an exit. I had two choices. One, I could continue the trail to the left and try to make it on the John Muir Trail. Two, I could take the trail to the right, get off the JMT, hike out around 7 miles alone to a parking lot, pickup, rest, recover, and a long drive home.

As I sat talking with God, Pastor Michael Haley arrived at the top of the trail. After a few moments chatting with him, I made the decision official: I would leave the JMT that day. He radioed ahead to tell someone to pick me up, and I headed off down the trail with my head hanging.

I made the 7-mile hike out alone, frustrated, a bit heart-broken, but with a quicker pace than any I had hiked thus far on the trail. Arriving at the parking lot, my ride was already there to get me to some much-needed recovery time.

Over the next few days, I got to spend time with several others who had planned to leave the hike early. I built friendships I pray will last a lifetime. I shrugged off the frustration and hurt a little. I can't tell you my time on the John Muir Trail was full of fun, but I can say I know, and trust God had me there for a reason. He brought me home for a reason. He leads me to continue to do what I do as my mission in life for many reasons. Some I know. Some only He knows. And that's okay with me.

Joey Candillo

Hiking the JMT was a life changing experience. It was by far the most physically challenging thing I have ever done. I am not an experienced hiker. When I was invited to go on this hike, I was hesitant at first. Honestly, I had to Google it because I had never heard of the John Muir Trail. I didn't think I could take that much time away from my church. However, I looked at this as an opportunity to help a lot of kids in poverty and I also was looking forward to the challenge. I wanted to see if I had the mental fortitude and to see if my body could hold up at 45 years old. I found in my absence, people from my church stepped up and took on certain leadership responsibilities. It was encouraging and a lesson in leadership.

Once I decided to go on this hike, I realized I didn't have any of the necessary gear. Everything needed to be super lightweight. Ultralight gear is expensive. I watched a lot of YouTube videos and gained a wealth of knowledge. I needed to train and get my body in shape. There are no mountains where I live so that proved to be difficult. I hit the gym every day and really felt prepared. However, there is no way to prepare for the altitude. Fortunately, I didn't have any problems with the altitude, but it did affect others in the group though. My biggest challenge turned out to be my food supply. Three months leading up to the hike I began doing the Keto diet. I lost a bunch of weight and was able to get into hiking shape. However, the food I packed was mostly Keto, which meant very few carbs and sugar. As a result, on about day four, I started to lose energy. Plus, consider I didn't have an appetite for the first three days because of the altitude. I barely choked down any food for the first few days. On day four, someone gave me a bit of their blueberry energy bar which triggered something in my taste buds. It gave me a boost in energy, and I couldn't get enough sugar. Fortunately, on day four. we got our food supply and most guys still had a lot of food left over. So, I left that resupply with a backpack full of energy bars and other high carb foods. I was set.

The JMT is physically grueling. At the end of each day, my feet hurt so badly, I just wanted to lay down as soon as I got into camp. Going downhill is murder on your feet. The constant pounding just takes a toll. Also, my backpack took a toll on my back. My sciatic nerve started hurting on day five and the rest of the time I couldn't feel the toes on my right foot. The worst thing happened on the last day. I woke up with a pain in my left shin. As we started hiking, it got progressively worse. Eventually, I realized I had shin splints from overexertion of my legs. By the time we got to the end on the last day, I could barely even walk. I literally limped in, but I made it. Such is life.

I learned several life lessons during the hike. The first lesson was about preparation. If you train well, the hike is enjoyable. If you don't train hard enough, the hike is miserable, and you may not finish. Another lesson was God is an amazing artist and I take His art for granted too often. It's sad we are oblivious to the marvel of creation. When you see all the mountains, you can see the creativity of God. I hope I never again take it for granted. Another lesson was about community. I'm so glad we did this as a team. Having good company makes all the difference in the world. It was great to be able to point at a mountain or lake and say, "look at that!" This experience taught me how important it is to do life with others. We encouraged each other during the hike. Sometimes we pushed each other. I believe God created us for community and having accountability is so vitally important.

Two people died on the JMT while we were hiking. We passed by a guy who had died five hours earlier. He tried to cross some snow early in the morning and he slipped and died instantly. He was in a body bag when we passed him. It was sad. He was hiking alone. After we finished the hike, we found out there was a woman who fell off Half Dome and died about the same time we passed by there. The JMT can be very dangerous and I'm thankful we didn't have any major injuries.

I will remember this hike the rest of my life. It created a love for hiking I could not have imagined. I long to go hiking regularly. I can't wait for the next challenge.

Lonnie Lehrman

When I was training for our adventure, I imagined I was going to have some major "ah-ha" moments. Now, don't get me wrong, God did teach me many things. I think the most surprising thing was I was going to lose my tent. Yes, you read that right. I lost my tent. Andrew and I had backpacked about five miles looking for Shawn, so the day was very long and emotional. Since we hiked five miles down a mountain the day before, we hiked ten before we started our 18.9-mile day. Little did I know Andrew was part mountain goat, as he flew up one of the steepest climbs, we had on our 17-day hike. This was the day we climbed the mountain containing the memorial Jon Muir Hut. Anyway, we were summiting this amazing mountain, we came across snow on the pass so we climbed a rocky area trying to miss the snow (you might be asking why I would include that detail.) Well, when we finally finished our marathon hike for the day, I realized I had lost my tent which was strapped to the bottom of my backpack. That was the beginning of my life lessons God was instilling in me.

For a few nights, I tried to get warm and comfortable, but to no avail. God started to whisper to me, "Now you know a little bit of what the kids feel like on an everyday basis." The difference was I knew I would be home in a couple of weeks, where comfort was normal. During those few short days God reminded me I was hungry, tired and cold. I was very emotional and even more driven to finish this hike, get back home and raise more money for these incredible kids we get to help through MANNA World-wide.

Austin (AKA Brown Sugar) Crow

They call me Brown Sugar. The story behind that
name will live in infamy, but I guess there are worse things
to be named after than a pop tart. Out of all the memories
made on the hike that one is at the top of my list. Because
I was there for a different reason than most, I walked away
with memories in a different form, video.

Originally, I joined the team with the sole purpose of
documenting the journey for marketing purposes. I work
for MANNA Worldwide full time as their Marketing Man-
ager, so naturally when something this big gets organized
for the purpose of raising money, the camera man auto-
matically gets signed up. I like camping and I enjoy the
outdoors. However, the last time I had gone on a hike, it
was 3 miles and I threw up at the end. Out of shape was an
understatement. I'm not saying I didn't want to go. I will
say though, mentally and physically, I was more unprepared than I could have possibly imagined.

When you think of hiking, you often think of a fun,
relaxing, enjoyable leisure activity. For me the hike was
excruciatingly painful (thanks to some of the worst foot
blisters I'll probably ever have in my life), filled with doubt
I would make it, thoughts of wishing I could go home, and
levels of physical exhaustion I have never experienced before. To top it off, I had to document every moment of

every day and somehow come out the end with something worth watching. Would I do it again? In a heartbeat. Alongside that pain was growth, with the exhaustion came rest in the most beautiful scenery I've ever seen on God's green earth. Above all, when you're cold, sleeping on the ground and tired beyond belief, it really puts in perspective how blessed we are to live the comfortable lives we do.

Lastly, I'd just like to say I'm extremely thankful for the extraordinary, Godly men and women in this book who made the trip more than just a physical feat. I truly believe I would not have finished if it wasn't for them. If you are considering a journey like this, please just know that you will not be the same. You will come out the other side a better version of yourself in more ways than you know.

P.S. Follow me on Instagram if you want to see my pictures from the hike! @austinecrow

Darrell "Butch" Ibach

It is impossible to put into words the experience I had while on the "Feed the Need" JMT trip.

The first question I think of is, "Why?" Why take months of training, 17 days away from family and work, while spending my own money on equipment, supplies and travel? For me, the answer is MANNA Worldwide' s mission statement to help children escape the grip of poverty. That was my answer and made it all worth it.

I went for that reason, but while on the trip, two things come to mind my mind repeatedly. First, we were a community of men and women who were doing this hike together. We needed each other to get through this and to the other end. This picture came most clear to me when Shawn and I fell way back from the group about 7 days into the trip. We were all tired, but Shawn was really feeling the cumulative effects from the previous days of hiking. He was struggling physically and mentally to continue. I knew if I didn't stay with him, he wasn't going to be able to make it through the day. He needed me at that time and TOGETHER we were going to make it! We hiked all day and late into the night. We arrived at camp hours after the rest of the group. We didn't eat. I didn't even undress for bed. I only took off my shoes and got into my sleeping bag and fell asleep. It was a brutally tough day.

The next morning came early. We were all feeling better because the day ahead was going to be a shorter hike of only 13 miles. We were only climbing a few thousand feet and I headed out without much thought of the previous day. It was a new day. I felt pretty good and started on the hike. I was seldom in the front of the pack of hikers. I was usually in the middle or the back. That day, I was in the middle of the pack. Mike, John, and I arrived at the camp in late afternoon. We were the last of the hikers to arrive except for Shawn. At that moment, I realized Shawn was by himself and knew it was not good he was alone. The day turned into night and my heart began to sink. I remembered the day before. I knew it was extremely difficult for him, but my prayer was he would arrive at camp ok because of the shorter hiking distance and only one mountain pass to conquer. I tried to convince myself he would make it.

Looking back now, I realize we needed each other throughout the trip. When Shawn was separated from the group, it wasn't good! We were designed to live in community, and I will always remember that in life.

Second, I was impacted by the truth we must not worry about tomorrow. It was interesting we all wanted to know, every morning, how far we had to go and how high we had to climb. There were days of 15 or 20 miles of hiking, and we had to climb six or seven thousand feet. We all knew we had a daunting task ahead of us. I got into mental trouble when I started to think about what was ahead of me, instead of what was right in front of me.

I remember thinking to myself, at the end of the first day, "I don't know if I can do this for 16 more days." Then I thought about something my son said to me before I left for the trip. "Dad, how do you eat a whale? One bite at a time." I thought to myself, I will make it through this . . . one step at a time. The Lord knew what He was talking about when He said not to worry about tomorrow because today has enough trouble of its own. That verse became very important to me on this trip and I hope to grow more into it as life continues.

Those were two valuable lessons that will always stick with me. But, the most important is thing is always, people. The people I got to know on this trip, for us to do this hike together, is what I will always cherish. Thanks for the memories to all were WITH me on the JMT!

Andrew Even

Pushing, expanding, and growing describe who I want to be and things I want to be doing. I want to strive for this to be true in all areas of my life: faith, family, body, mind, relationships and influence in the world.

I've always loved the outdoors and hiking. I was blessed to grow up in two places with beautiful mountain ranges, California and Chile, as well as having a geologist as a father who loves all things rock. I'd grown up learning about John Muir in school and hiking with family and friends in the Sierra Nevada, mostly in Yosemite. As I began to dream over a year ago about tackling a longer distance trail, my attention and research quickly focused on the John Muir Trail. I started sharing my longing for this adventure with a few friends and to my surprise they got excited about the idea too. The opportunity to achieve something physical, while impacting others in need, was a draw we couldn't pass up. We could raise money for hungry kids. Reaching these kids and their communities all over the world by sharing the love of Jesus with them, is the thing I've given my life to do. We could also use this training group of friends to work into better physical shape and toughen our focus mentally. On top of it all, it would provide stories, brotherhood and a ton of fun. I was nervous that no one would fully commit to the challenge, but

I was humbled that friends caught the vision and jumped on board enthusiastically.

Over the next year we began to prepare ourselves for the hike. While difficult, it was so enjoyable working individually and collectively towards our goal and being ready to start the hike. We planned out every detail, researching our gear, preparing our food and arranging our logistics. This was only to get to the starting point. I came to appreciate several things during this time. First, that the preparation, planning and anticipation were a huge part of the joy and satisfaction. Second, people watching us will also respond, get behind, and give toward the cause, being inspired by those who demonstrate their heart and passion for the needy and willingness to sacrifice to achieve their goal. Lastly, men crave adventure and challenge.

The 17-day thru-hike was all I could have asked for and more. It was the hardest physical challenge I've ever done, but so grateful I got to accomplish this big goal. Both the painfully difficult moments and the exhilarating moments were a blessing. I've learned this is true in all areas of life. It makes me think of these words by Tauren Wells in his song, "Hills and Valleys."

On the mountains I will bow my life to the One who set me there

In the valley I will lift my eyes to the One who
sees me there

When I'm standing on the mountain, I didn't get
there on my own

When I'm walking through the valley, I know I
am not alone

You're God of the hills and valleys[1]

While hiking, I carried a set of laminated pictures
clipped onto my pack. The pictures were of kids at our orphanage in Guatemala with their beautiful smiles, holding
handmade signs of encouragement and motivation. There
were pictures of kids at our feeding center in Tijuana,
Mexico, who had stolen my heart. I had pictures of my
family, who I knew were praying for me, had encouraged
me in all my training, and were sacrificing time away from
me for us to accomplish this goal. The goals being providing kids' food, a home, education, discipleship and loving
care. Every time I was tired or discouraged or struggling,
these pictures were there to remind me in those valleys
why I was doing this and for who I was taking another step
forward.

[1] Jonathan Smith, Tauren Wells, and Chuck Butler, "Hills and Valleys," 2017.

During the brief moments we were able to get an internet connection, we were blown away by the way people were responding to our updates and photos. So many donations were pouring in, along with messages of encouragement. Some people were even motivated to take on their own challenge during this time to stretch themselves to a new level.

The simplicity of life on the trail was something I'll treasure. Being singularly focused with a simple goal of getting up and walking every day was tremendously renewing. You couldn't think too far ahead on all the miles that remained because it was too far out and overwhelming. Accomplishing the miles and the mountain passes for that day was my only focus. We were on this journey long enough that this way of life had to be embraced as a new normal far from our ordinary life. I had never really experienced this before, because on most trips within a few days of being in an unfamiliar place, you just think to yourself it will only be another few days and I'll be back home again. In order to make it, I had to adapt my mind to fully embrace this lifestyle as my new reality. This simplicity was liberating and gave me a sense of peace.

One of the beautiful highlights for me was being surprised by my wife, Angie, at the end of the trail in Yosemite Valley. It's a feeling I won't ever forget. Somehow, she had arranged a flight out to California and driven up with my parents from San Diego, who were generously helping our team with transportation logistics. I'm blessed to have a wife who enjoys adventure and a challenge, is just as dedicated to our cause, and is unwaveringly supportive of me. I'm so thankful to all the spouses and families who sacrificed for this goal.

I had asked God from the get-go to use this experience to transform me and come out of it as a 2.0 version of myself. This way I could serve Him in a way that would maximize the purpose He has for the second half of my life. I believe I'm now stronger in my faith, determination, confidence and physical stamina. I pray I can now be used to bring more glory to God because of His work in me.

I'm so grateful for being able to take this journey from start to finish. I'm thankful God allowed me to experience it all. I'm so appreciative of all our followers who prayed for us and gave sacrificially for our $100,000 goal to be achieved. To our #FeedTheNeed team, words can't fully describe all we experienced to those who were not on this journey, but we know, and our bond is something I will be forever grateful for. I'm honored to have walked with you.

MOUNTAIN MOMENTS
Photos by @AustinECrow

Cottonwood Lakes—The Adventure Begins

View from the Top of Mt. Whitney

Northern side of Forester Pass

Evolution Lake

Palisade Creek

Lake Virginia

Yosemite National Park

Yosemite National Park

El Capitan

Yosemite National Park

Nevada Falls

Garnet Lake

Bear Creek

Northern Side of Selden Pass

Southern Side of Pinchot Pass

Rae Lakes

Northern Side of New Army Pass

The Finish Line

I have watched families lose the battle for their families for far too long. Satan is winning the battle against the family and to say I am frustrated is grossly understated. I desire parents to become passionate in the fight for their family. That is the purpose of this book. I pray parents will decide their kids are worth the fight. I pray dads will take a stand and quit observing from the sidelines. Unfortunately, most of us are taking our cues from Adam. Adam passively sat next to Eve as the serpent engaged her in the fight for her life. Adam did nothing. Adam failed to fight. Adam failed to protect. Adam failed his family. I pray this book will inspire, challenge, and equip you to step in the ring and fight.

Too many times we pray for God to do a miracle, but we are not willing to make a move to meet Him halfway. As you read this book, my prayer is you will be challenged and encouraged to make the necessary moves in your life to be prepared for breakthrough, if God chooses to breakthrough in your life.

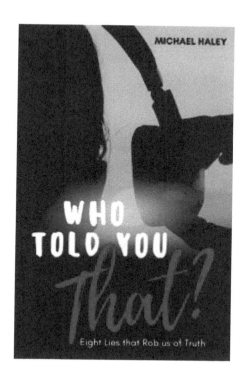

Since the beginning of creation, Satan has been lying to God's children to keep them from being the child God has created them to be. As you read this book, my prayer is you will be reminded of the truths of God and have a greater desire to fight against the lies of Satan which rob us of those truths.